ARCHITECTURAL DELINEATION

ARCHITECTURAL DELINEATION

PROFESSIONAL SHORTCUTS

IVO D. DRPIC

VNR VAN NOSTRAND REINHOLD COMPANY
_____ New York

To my beloved wife, Consuelito

Printed in Hong Kong

Van Nostrand Reinhold Company Inc.
115 Fifth Avenue
New York, New York 10003

Van Nostrand Reinhold Company Limited
Molly Millars Lane
Wokingham, Berkshire RG11 2PY, England

Van Nostrand Reinhold
480 La Trobe Street
Melbourne, Victoria 3000, Australia

Macmillan of Canada
Division of Canada Publishing Corporation
164 Commander Boulevard
Agincourt, Ontario M1S 3C7, Canada

16 15 14 13 12 11 10 9 8 7 6 5 4 3 2 1

Library of Congress Cataloging-in-Publication Data

Drpic, Ivo D.
    Architectural delineation.

    1. Architectural drawing—Technique. I. Title.
NA2708.D77 1988   720′.28′4   87-34502
ISBN 0-442-22105-3

1415 Louisiana United Bank Plaza—Houston, Texas.
Developer: Wortham & Van Liew. Architect: M. Nasr &
Partners, P.C. Colored markers and nylon-tip pen. 6″
× 10″. 1 hour.

Contents

Office Tower—Houston, Texas. Architect: Ivo D. Drpic &
Associates. Colored markers and nylon-tip pen. 8″ × 6½″.
10 minutes.

Foreword

Architectural drawings are the primary tools for developing ideas and recording thoughts during the early stages of the creative process. With each stroke of the pencil, brush, or felt pen, the designer examines alternatives and brings his or her vision into clearer focus. Whether an idea is accepted or rejected depends, to a large extent, on the designer's ability to sketch effectively.

The imaginative drawing technique illustrated in Ivo Drpic's book frees the designer's mind and stimulates his or her thoughts. Drpic's effective technique eliminates superfluous detail to reveal the essence of a concept. His handsome illustrations prove that hand drawing is the best way to record the conceptual design process and communicate the intrinsic beauty of the designer's vision.

Earle S. Alexander, FAIA
Pierce Goodwin Alexander
Houston, Texas

Office Tower—Dallas, Texas. Architect: Ivo D. Drpic & Associates. Sketch by Geraldine Drpic. Colored markers and felt-tip pen. 5″ × 4½″. 30 minutes.

Preface

Architectural delineation is an effective means of transferring ideas and concepts to paper. In addition to sharpening an architect's vision and promoting an exchange of ideas in the professional office, a revised perspective sketch can serve as an effective sales tool, offering the client a detailed study of the proposed project.

Although some professionals believe that perspectives, or three-dimensional drawings, can be misleading and are useful mainly as selling devices, Frank Lloyd Wright, Le Corbusier, Oscar Niemayer, Paul Rudolph, Hugh Stubbins, and Quincy Jones all found sketches useful in their work. It is my belief that an architect who masters the art of sketching will produce more sophisticated designs.

The skills necessary for producing effective sketches are difficult, but not impossible to master. *Architectural Delineation* includes tips on sketching, step-by-step demonstrations, and a wide-ranging portfolio of architectural sketches. With some discipline and dedication, this book offers all that is needed to proceed from simple sketches to finished drawings.

Office Tower—Houston, Texas. Architect: Ivo D. Drpic & Associates. Colored markers and nylon-tip pen. 9¼″ × 6¼″. 12 minutes.

Acknowledgments

I owe a great debt to my father, the late Antonio Drpic, who was my mentor and inspiration, and to my mother, Susy Drpic, who offered constant support. I would like to thank my wife, Consuelito, for her love, help, and encouragement, and my daughters, Jeancarla, Giovanna, and Geraldine, for their contributions.

I would also like to extend my thanks to Hy Applebaum, who supplied the information for left-handed people; Earle Alexander, for his contributions; Wendy Lochner, Linda Venator, and Donna Rossler at Van Nostrand Reinhold, for their valuable advice; and my clients.

J. Ray McDermott Office Complex—Houston, Texas. Project Architects: Jack M. Reber, Ivo D. Drpic. Colored markers and nylon-tip pen. 8″ × 3″. 15 minutes.

PART I

INTRODUCTION
TO SKETCHING

1. SKETCHES

Sketches are the means by which architects, designers, and interior designers translate their ideas, thoughts, and concepts to paper.

An effective sketch conveys a particular feeling about its subject. Creating such a sketch requires thought as well as physical dexterity, which can be acquired with sufficient practice. The knowledge of perspective is necessary to achieve a three-dimensional effect with textures, patterns, colors, and shadows.

Sketches are invaluable tools for initiating design projects, because—unlike models and final renderings—sketches can be executed quickly, they are easy to alter, and they are inexpensive.

A *thumbnail sketch* is usually very small and consists of few lines. It is used to capture a specific idea or look, explain some architectural detail, or study a particular angle in a perspective. Thumbnail sketches generally precede a more detailed drawing.

Thumbnail sketch of vacation home—Houston, Texas. Architect: Ivo D. Drpic & Associates. Colored markers and nylon-tip pen. 7″ × 4″. 5 minutes.

As the name implies, a *medium-detail sketch* includes textures and shades to introduce more details.

A *finished sketch* is generally an elaboration of a thumbnail or medium-detail sketch. Color is applied to a finished sketch and an airbrush is often used for touchups.

BEROL PM 35
SPANISH OLIVE

BEROL PM 104
WARM GRAY

BEROL PM 48
NON-PHOTO BLUE

IVO DRPIC

BEROL PM 27
APPLE GREEN

BEROL PM 94
DARK TAN

Medium-detail sketch of vacation home in Houston, Texas. Architect: Ivo D. Drpic & Associates. Colored markers and nylon-tip pen. 8″ × 5″. 15 minutes.

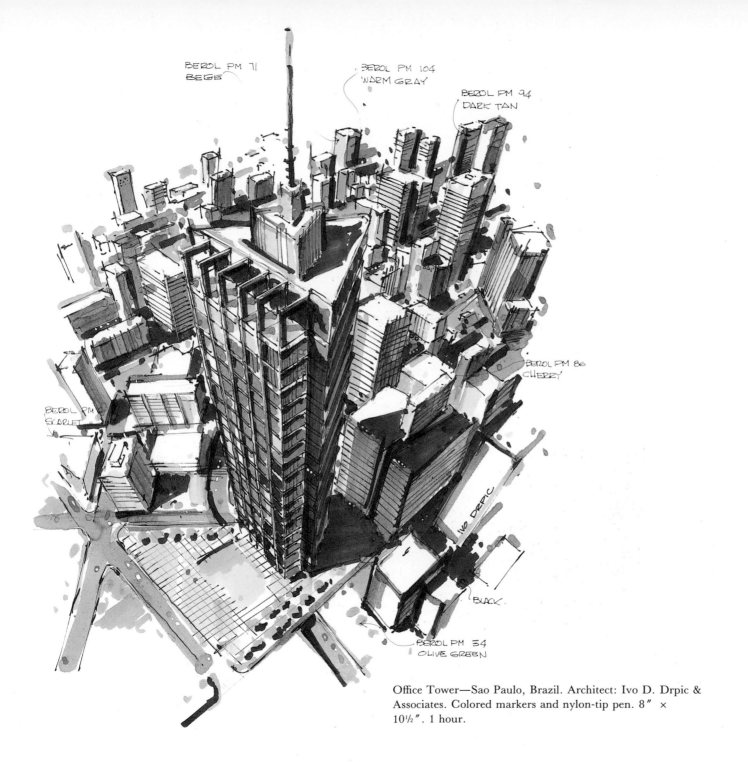

BEROL PM 71 BEIGE

BEROL PM 104 WARM GRAY

BEROL PM 94 DARK TAN

BEROL PM 86 CHERRY

BEROL PM SCARLET

IVO DRPIC

BLACK.

BEROL PM 34 OLIVE GREEN

Office Tower—Sao Paulo, Brazil. Architect: Ivo D. Drpic & Associates. Colored markers and nylon-tip pen. 8″ × 10½″. 1 hour.

2. EQUIPMENT

Paper

Sketching equipment should be kept to a minimum. The necessary tools include sketch paper and black and color markers. The rolls of sketch paper used for the illustrations in this text are Dietzgen and Keuffel & Esser. These come in widths of 12, 18, 24, 30, and 36 inches and effectively hold the color of markers. Felt-

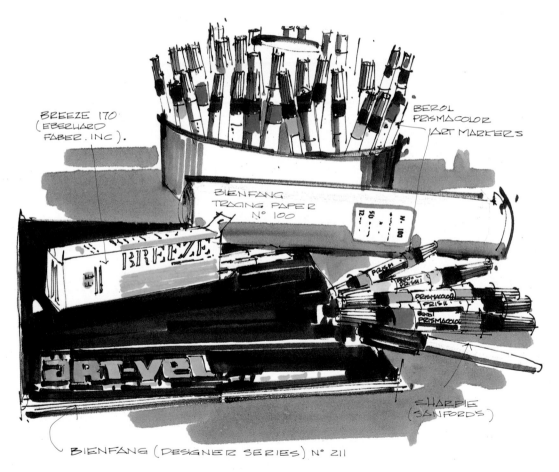

Equipment. Private Residence—New Braunfels, Texas.
Architect: Ivo D. Drpic & Associates.

tip pens (fine, medium, and broad) run smoothly across the paper. Sketches completed on this paper can be dry mounted and become part of a more permanent presentation.

Sketch pads are manageable and therefore good for working outdoors. They produce less permanent results, since the colors of markers tend to fade.

Sketchbooks are also efficient for work outdoors, but these do not allow for overlays.

Markers

The Breeze 170 nylon-tip pen is good for initial sketches and for final lines and touch-ups. The pen is lightweight, inexpensive, and does not produce diluted colors.

The Sharpie pen is ideal for large drawings, for touch-ups, and for adding definition. The Berol Prismacolor Art Marker PM-98 Black is ideal for filling large areas of black.

Berol Prismacolor, Pantone Letraset, and Eberhard Faber Design are reputable brands of colored art markers. I prefer the Berol Prismacolor, since each marker has two different tips, and the effects of each mix well. It is generally unnecessary to buy a complete set of markers, with ninety-six or more colors. It is best to keep a large supply of the colors used most frequently, since markers will get dirty or dry out after a few sketches and will then be useful only for special effects.

Recommended Berol Prismacolor Markers

PM	2	Chinese Red	PM	78	Brick Beige
PM	3	Crimson Lake	PM	80	Putty
PM	5	Scarlet Lake	PM	84	Bark
PM	7	Lipstick Red	PM	85	Mahogany
PM	18	Cadmium Yellow	PM	86	Cherry
			PM	89	Light Walnut
PM	27	Apple Green	PM	95	Light Tan
PM	34	Olive Green	PM	98	Black
PM	36	Lime Green	PM	99	Warm Gray— 10%
PM	38	Teal Blue			
PM	39	Process Blue	PM	100	Warm Gray— 20%
PM	41	Fathom Blue			
PM	42	Flag Blue	PM	101	Warm Gray— 30%
PM	46	Holiday Blue			
PM	47	Light Blue	PM	102	Warm Gray— 40%
PM	48	Non-Photo Blue	PM	103	Warm Gray— 50%
PM	49	Blue Violet			
PM	51	Grape	PM	104	Warm Gray— 60%
PM	52	Cranberry			
PM	59	Lavender	PM	105	Warm Gray— 70%
PM	64	Sienna Brown			
PM	65	Terra Cotta	PM	106	Warm Gray— 80%
PM	71	Beige			
PM	72	Ivory	PM	107	Warm Gray— 90%
PM	73	Flagstone Red			
PM	77	Dark Brick Red			

PART II

TIPS ON
SKETCHING

3☐ **DRAWING EXERCISES**

Drawing skills can be acquired and sharpened with practice. The following exercises serve to enhance eye-hand coordination, allowing the sketcher to represent effectively his or her thoughts on paper.

Left-handed individuals should reverse the process indicated wherever an asterisk appears.

Exercise 1*
Locate points A and B as shown.
Place your pen at A and your eyes at B.
Draw a straight line from point A, while looking at point B. Repeat this exercise until you have complete command of it.

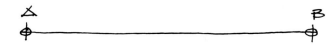

Exercise 2
Draw a series of horizontal parallel lines, keeping the distance between lines constant.

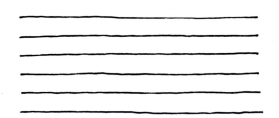

Exercise 3
Draw a series of vertical parallel lines, keeping the distance between lines constant.

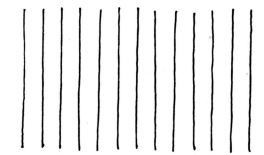

Exercise 4*
Draw a series of diagonal lines from bottom to top, keeping the distance between lines constant.

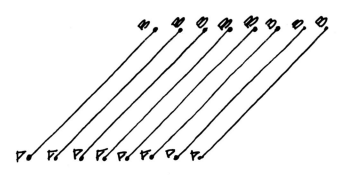

11

Exercise 5
Repeat the preceding exercises many times, gradually
reducing the distance between lines.

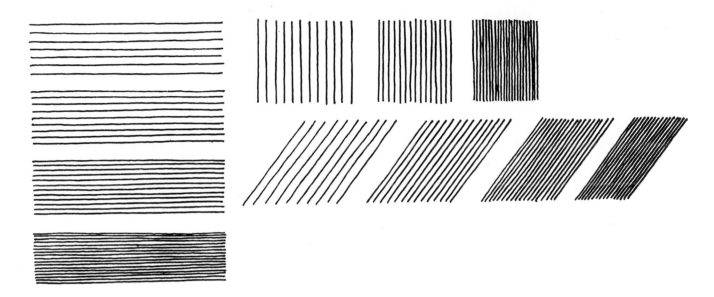

Exercise 6
Combine lines as shown below.
Create your own combinations.

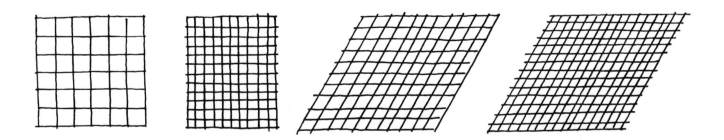

Exercise 7
Draw the geometric shapes shown below, and continue
drawing them until you can reproduce them effortlessly.

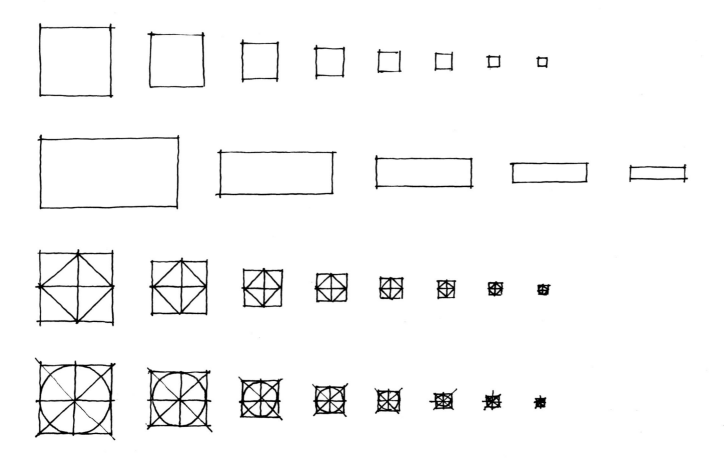

Exercise 8

Draw the three-dimensional objects shown, gradually reducing them. Then draw the small shapes and gradually enlarge them.

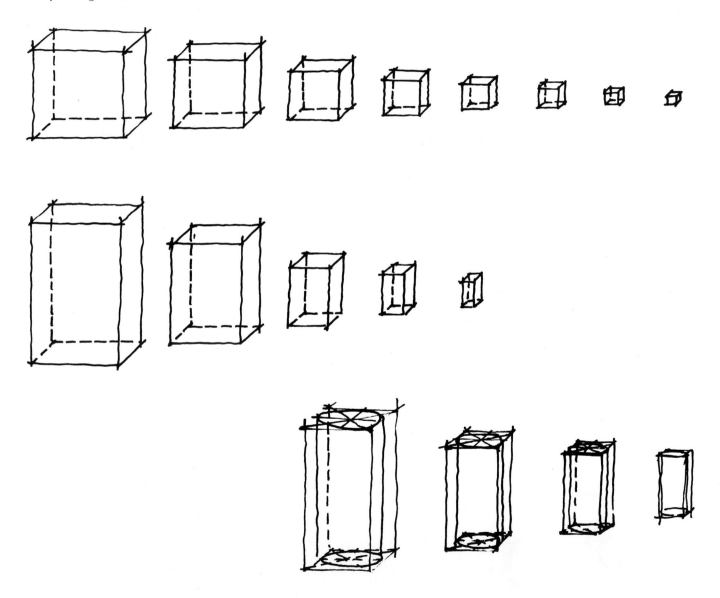

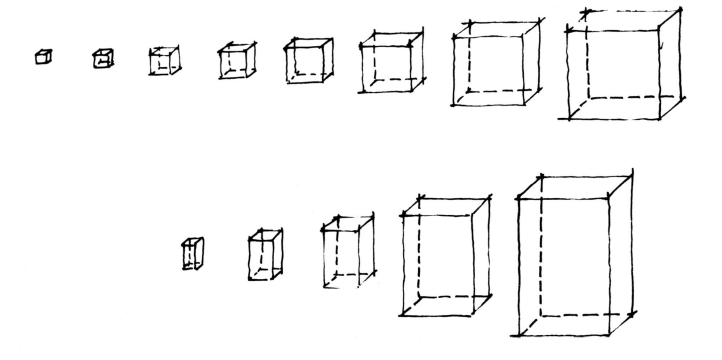

Exercise 9
Draw a cube and the various odd shapes illustrated,
showing different positions and sizes.

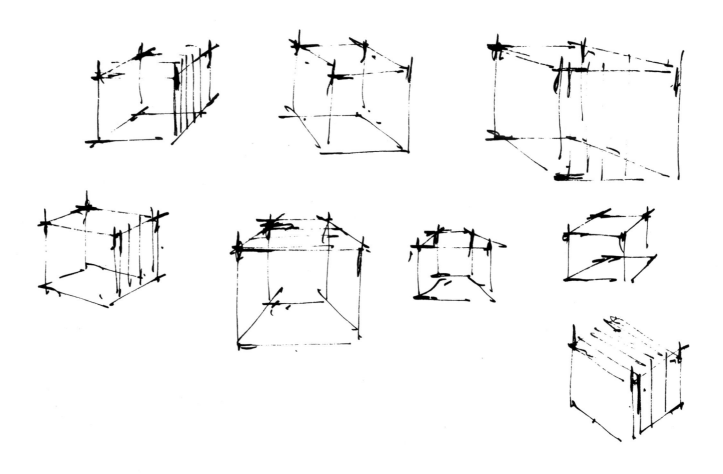

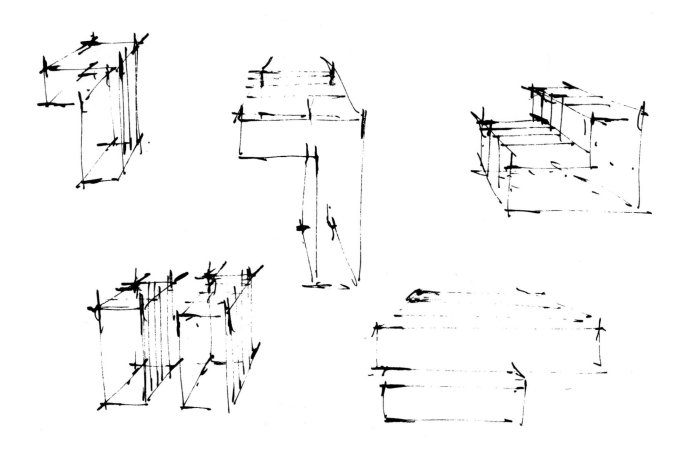

4. PERSPECTIVE EXERCISES

Perspective is the technique of altering the spatial relationships between objects on a plane or curved surface to approximate the way we actually see these objects in space.

Freehand perspective drawings are design tools. Mechanical perspectives are much more complex and cannot be used in the design stage, since they are based on final plan and elevation drawings.

Perspective drawings are converging line projections and are classified as one, two, or three point, depending upon the number of points at which lines converge.

First draw a simple form, a cube in one-point perspective. Next, extend the edges of the cube as shown in the figure and notice that projection lines a, b, c, and d converge at a common point 0, called the *vanishing point*. The vanishing point always falls on the horizon.

Notice that sides $\overline{AB}$, $\overline{EF}$, and $\overline{GH}$ are parallel to the horizon in this case.

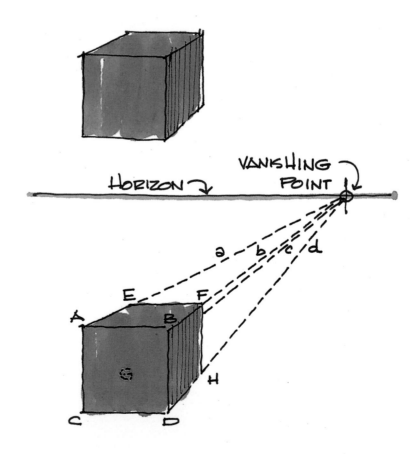

From this point on the horizon, all projections in one-point perspective—to the right, left, up, and down—are represented in the following scheme. Assuming that every cube is a simple building, this scheme would allow the reader to visualize, almost immediately, the angle or view of the building to be drawn.

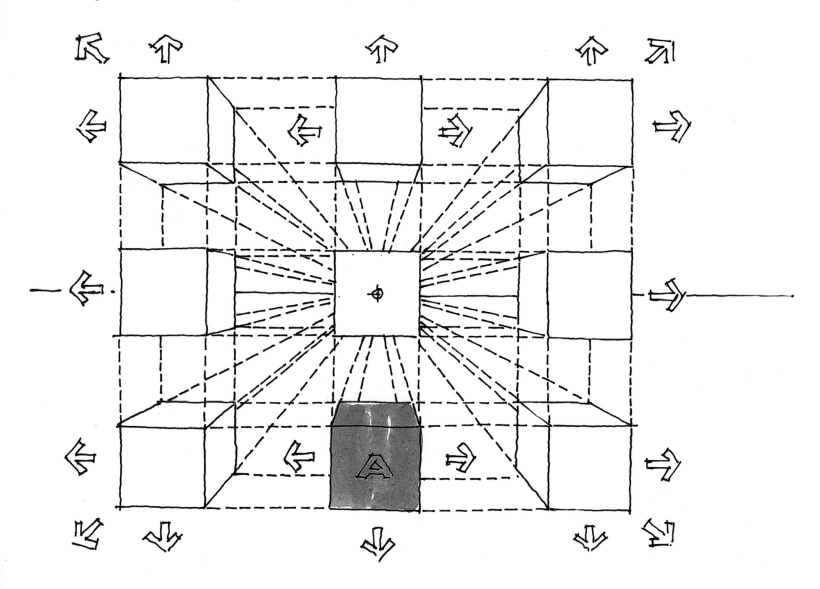

Next, draw a cube in two-point perspective. Extend the edges $\overline{AB}$, $\overline{CD}$, $\overline{EF}$, $\overline{GH}$, and $\overline{CA}$, $\overline{DB}$, $\overline{GE}$, $\overline{HF}$ as shown. Notice that the projections converge at two points located on the horizon line.

The following scheme shows the same cube represented in new positions.

From the above diagram, we can determine that

- vertical edges of a cube are always parallel; and
- space between vanishing points 1 and 2 will affect the elevations of the cube and the depth perspective.

Reproduce this diagram until it becomes familiar. Explore new forms by changing the distance between vanishing points. Again, take forms that were used in one-point perspectives and make them fit this scheme.

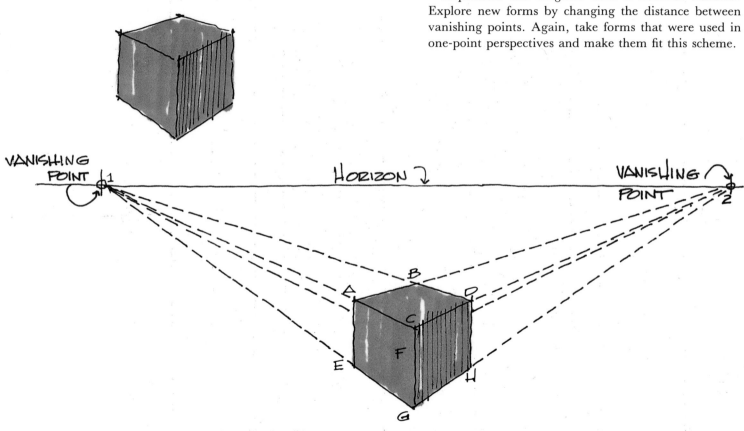

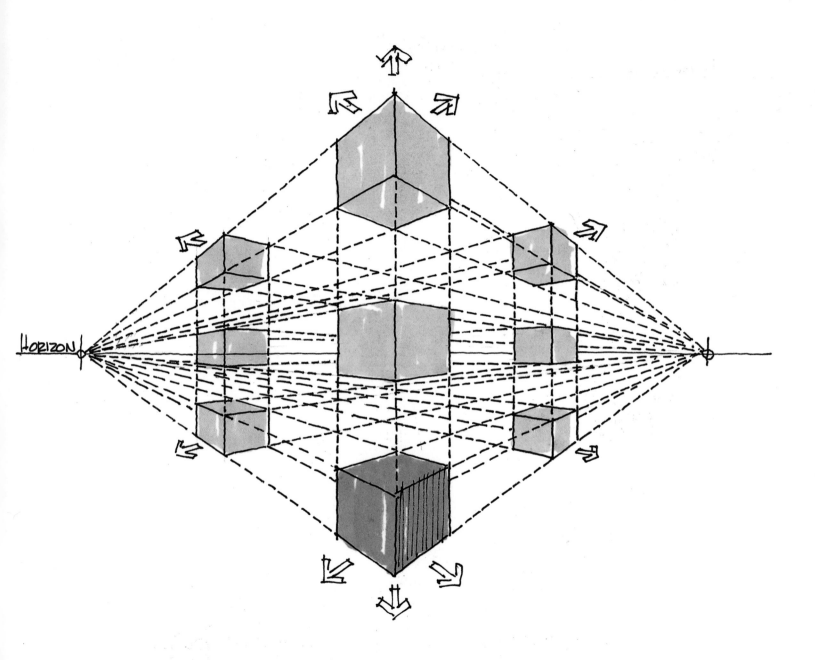

HORIZON

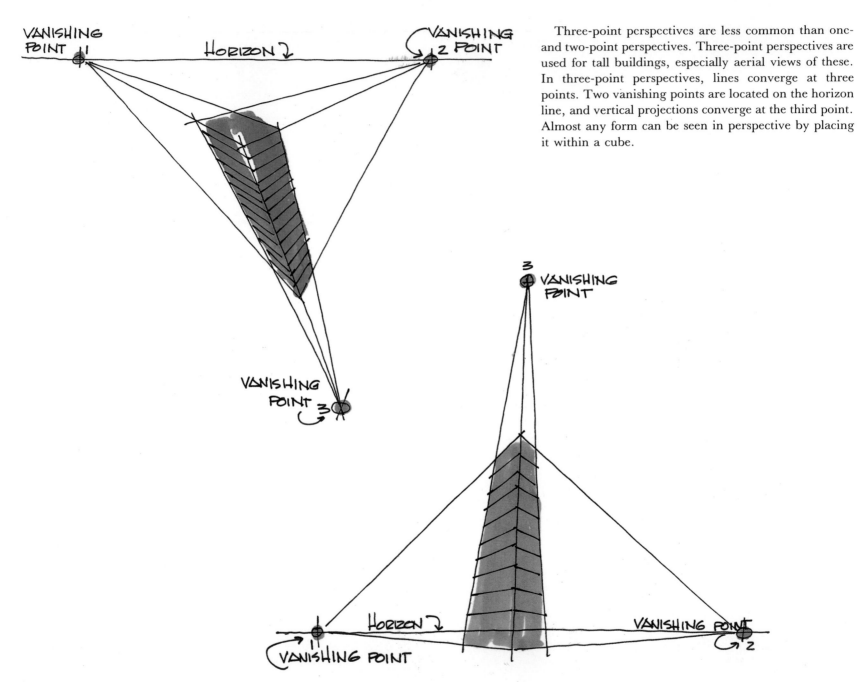

VANISHING POINT 1

HORIZON

VANISHING 2 POINT

VANISHING POINT 3

Three-point perspectives are less common than one- and two-point perspectives. Three-point perspectives are used for tall buildings, especially aerial views of these. In three-point perspectives, lines converge at three points. Two vanishing points are located on the horizon line, and vertical projections converge at the third point. Almost any form can be seen in perspective by placing it within a cube.

3 VANISHING POINT

HORIZON

VANISHING POINT 1

VANISHING POINT 2

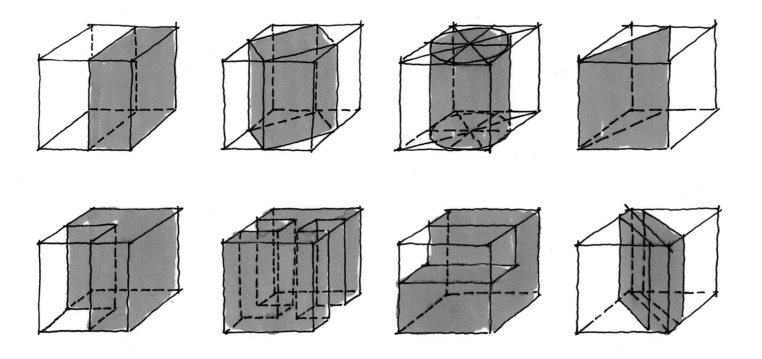

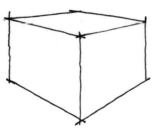

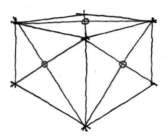

The Perspective Center

It is often necessary to find the center of building elevations in order to position certain elements, such as doors and windows. To find the perspective center of the sides of cubes, draw the diagonals, as shown in the accompanying illustrations. The point at which the diagonals intersect is the perspective center for that side of the cube.

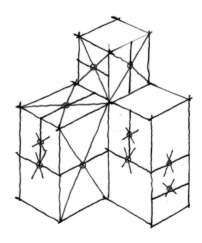

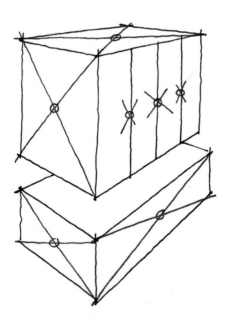

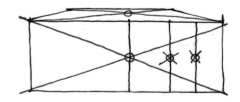

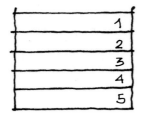

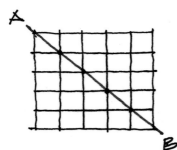

Perspective Spacing

This is the procedure by which the sides of geometric shapes are proportionally divided. Equally divide the side of a cube horizontally as shown, and then draw diagonal $\overline{AB}$.

To draw the cube in perspective, draw diagonals $\overline{AB}$ and $\overline{CA}$ and vertical lines at the points where the diagonals intersect the horizontal lines. Vertical spaces will be in the correct perspective.

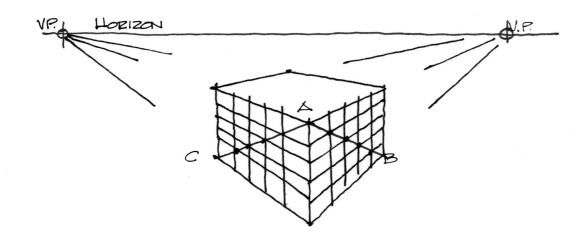

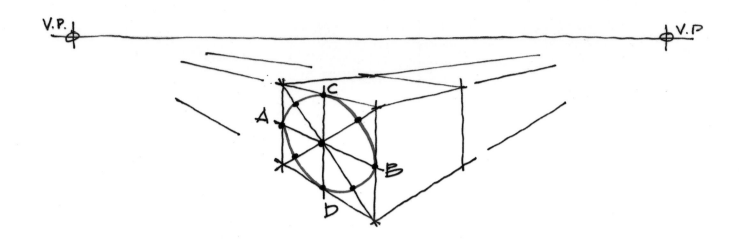

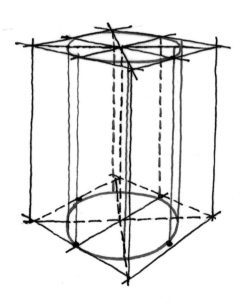

The Circle in Perspective

The circle in perspective is an ellipse. To create an ellipse, begin with a cube in two-point perspective. Draw diagonals on one side of the cube. The point at which the diagonals cross represents the center of the circle. Draw lines AB and CD and then the ellipse.

The Cylinder in Perspective

A rectangle in perspective is necessary for creating such a cylinder. Within a rectangular block, perspective squares are created; ellipses are then drawn within these squares, resulting in a cylinder.

Equal Spacing in Perspective

Draw two columns and add lines connecting the tops and bottoms of the columns with the vanishing point (V.P.). Draw a diagonal that extends from the top of the first column through the center of the second col-umn and ends at the bottom line. A vertical line should be drawn where the diagonal meets the line extending from the bottom of the column to the vanishing point. This will indicate the location of the new column. This process can be repeated to find the correct location for additional columns in perspective.

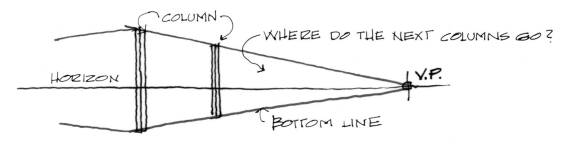

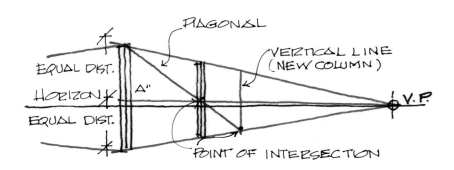

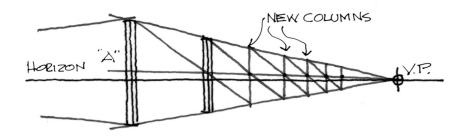

5. THE SIMPLIFIED USE OF SHADOWS

The samples of shadows cast by different shapes onto different surfaces show some common ways in which shadows are represented in sketches and renderings.

Observe the way that the sun casts shadows on different objects throughout the day.

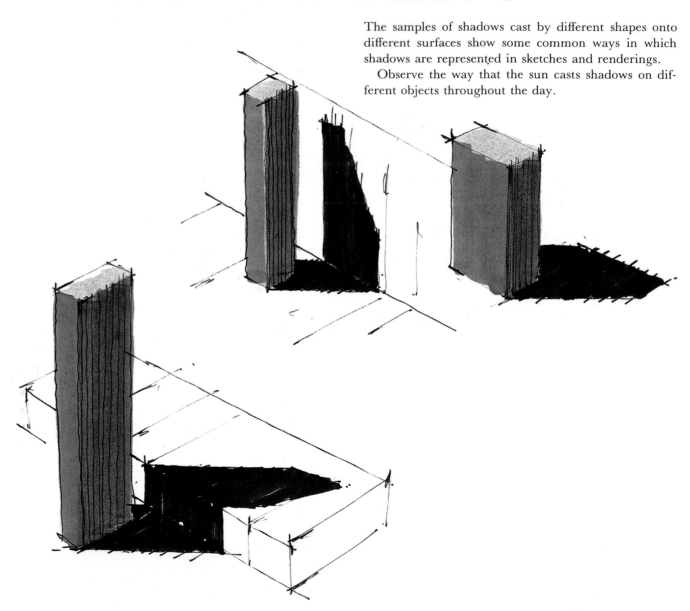

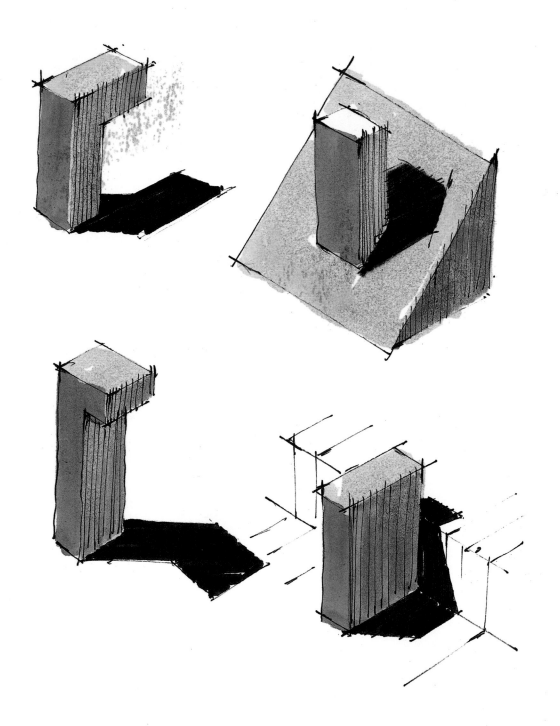

The Simplified Use of Shadows 29

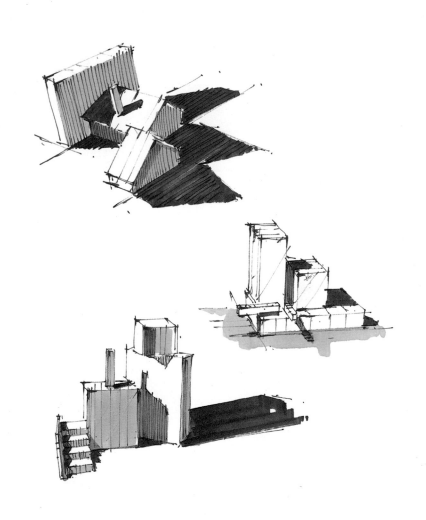

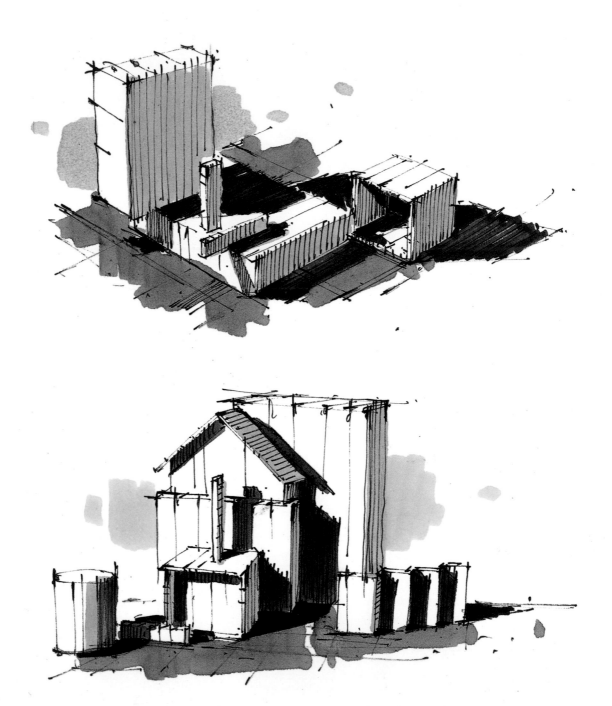

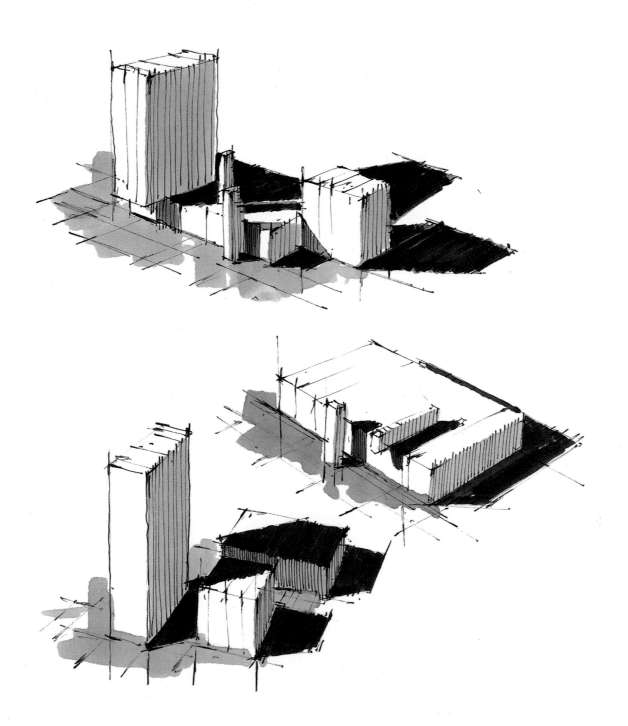

PART III

DEMONSTRATIONS OF SKETCH PREPARATION

6. DEMONSTRATION ONE

Aerial View of a Shopping Center

An aerial view of a project is generally taken when details (such as the limits of the property, roof, building, and parking configuration) must be represented. Simple projects generally call for an eye-level view. Aerial views, however, tend to show too much roof area—a less important aspect, since buildings are not usually seen from above.

Demonstration One shows two aerial views (with the

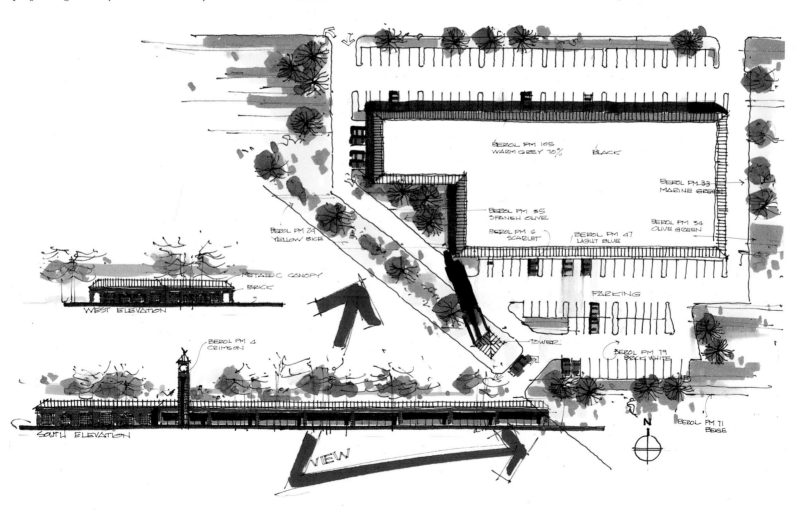

same vanishing points) of the same buildings. The second sketch, however, succeeds in minimizing the roof area by bringing the building closer to the horizon line.

Re-create the illustrations.

1. Draw the horizon line.
2. Roughly locate vanishing points 1, 2, 3, and 4.
3. Block the building with fast pen strokes.
4. Apply colors in the order indicated by numbers.
5. Polish details.

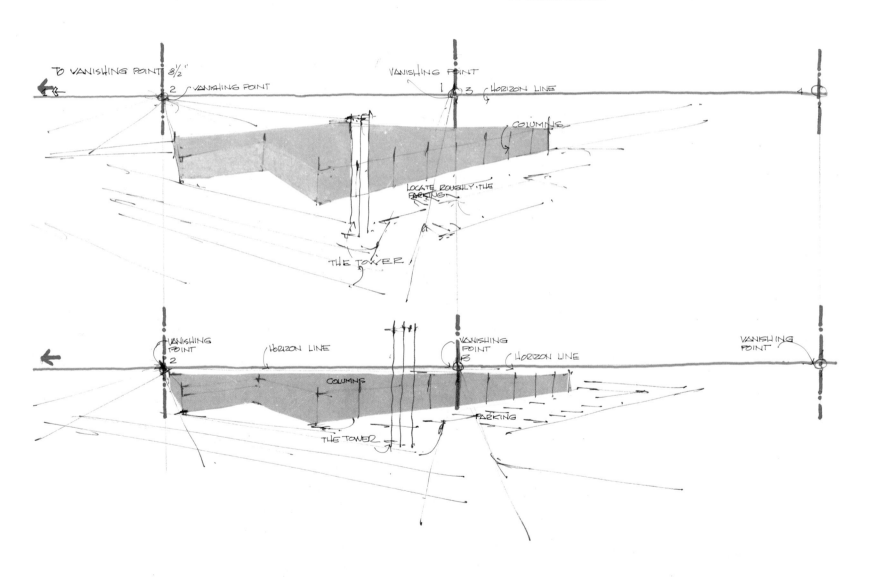

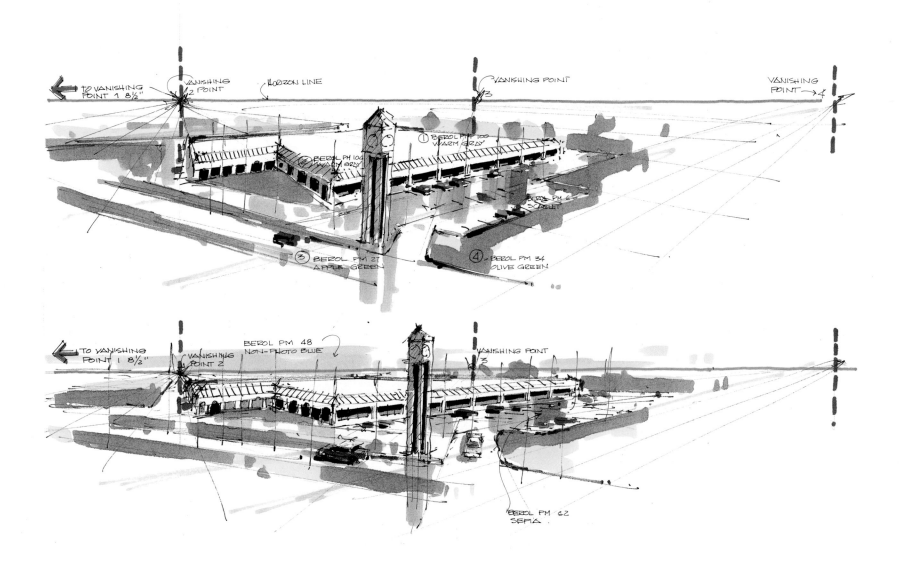

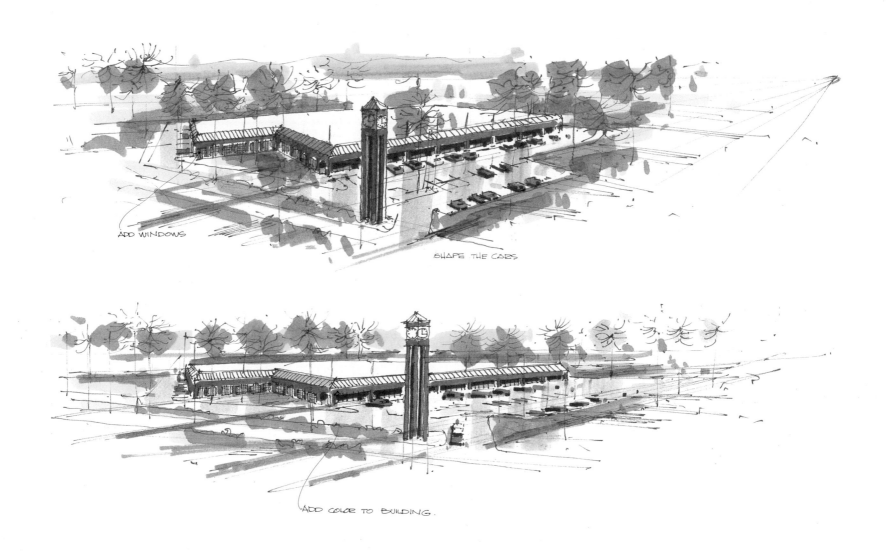

ADD WINDOWS

SHAPE THE CARS

ADD COLOR TO BUILDING.

7. DEMONSTRATION TWO

A Group of High-Rise Buildings

This demonstration consists of an eye-level view and a simple aerial view. Groups of buildings are represented as if seen from a distance (as blocks or masses).

View 1

1. Select the type of perspective (this is an eye-level view, or one-point perspective).
2. Locate the horizon line.
3. Locate the vanishing point.
4. Quickly position building masses and streets (no details).
5. Check the proportions.
6. Apply colors as indicated.

View 2

1. Select the type of perspective (this is an aerial view, or two-point perspective).

2. Locate the horizon line.
3. Locate the vanishing points.
4. Quickly position building masses and streets (no details).
5. Check proportions.
6. Apply colors as indicated.

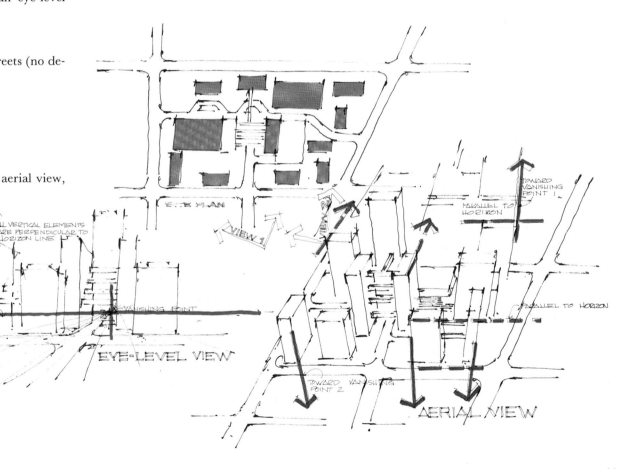

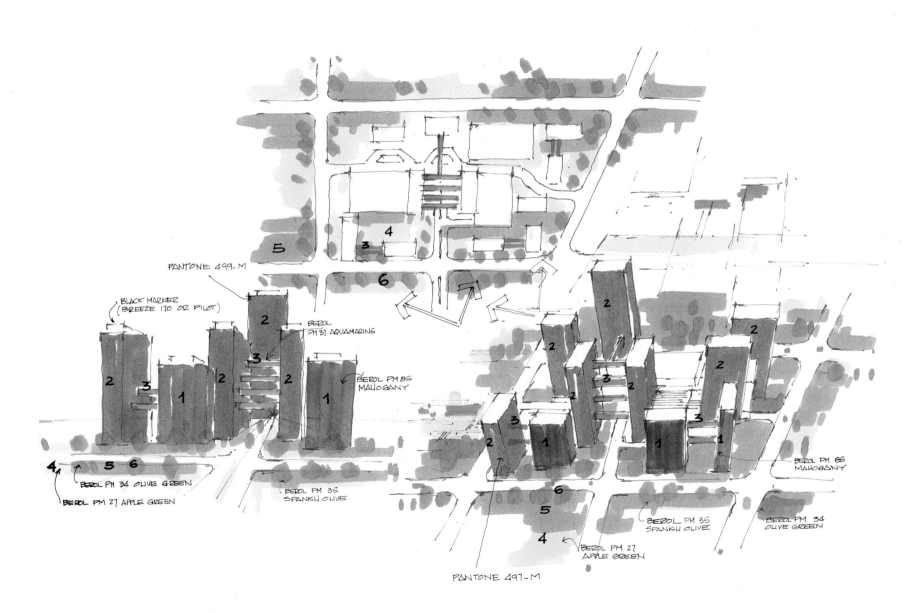

PANTONE 499-M

BLACK MARKER
(BREEZE 170 OR PILOT)

BEROL
PM 37 AQUAMARINE

BEROL PM 86
MAHOGANY

BEROL PM 34 OLIVE GREEN

BEROL PM 27 APPLE GREEN

BEROL PM 35
SPANISH OLIVE

BEROL PM 86
MAHOGANY

BEROL PM 35
SPANISH OLIVE

BEROL PM 34
OLIVE GREEN

BEROL PM 27
APPLE GREEN

PANTONE 497-M

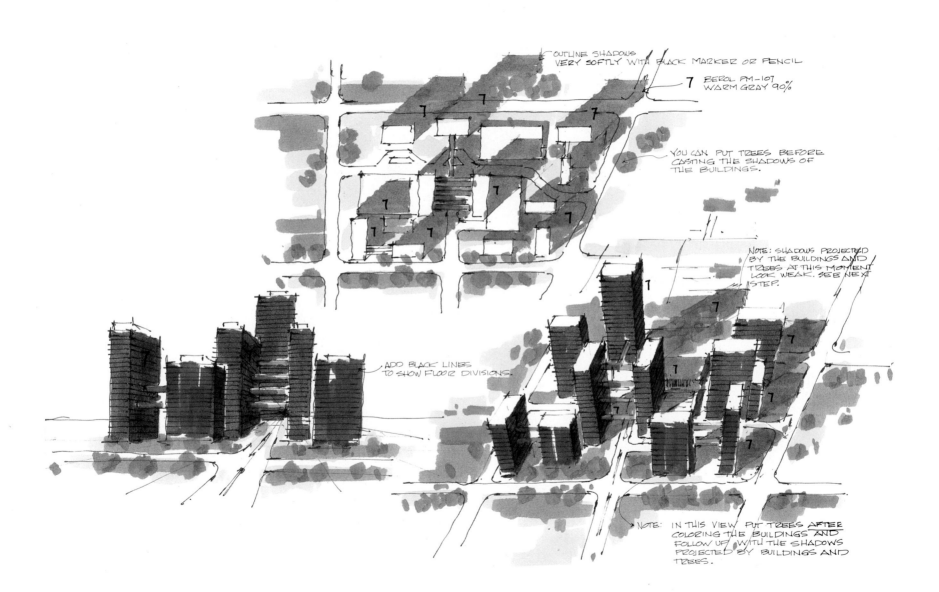

OUTLINE SHADOWS
VERY SOFTLY WITH BLACK MARKER OR PENCIL

7 BEROL PM-107
WARM GRAY 90%

YOU CAN PUT TREES BEFORE
CASTING THE SHADOWS OF
THE BUILDINGS.

NOTE: SHADOWS PROJECTED
BY THE BUILDINGS AND
TREES AT THIS MOMENT
LOOK WEAK. SEE NEXT
STEP.

ADD BLACK LINES
TO SHOW FLOOR DIVISIONS.

NOTE: IN THIS VIEW PUT TREES AFTER
COLORING THE BUILDINGS AND
FOLLOW UP WITH THE SHADOWS
PROJECTED BY BUILDINGS AND
TREES.

Demonstration Two 43

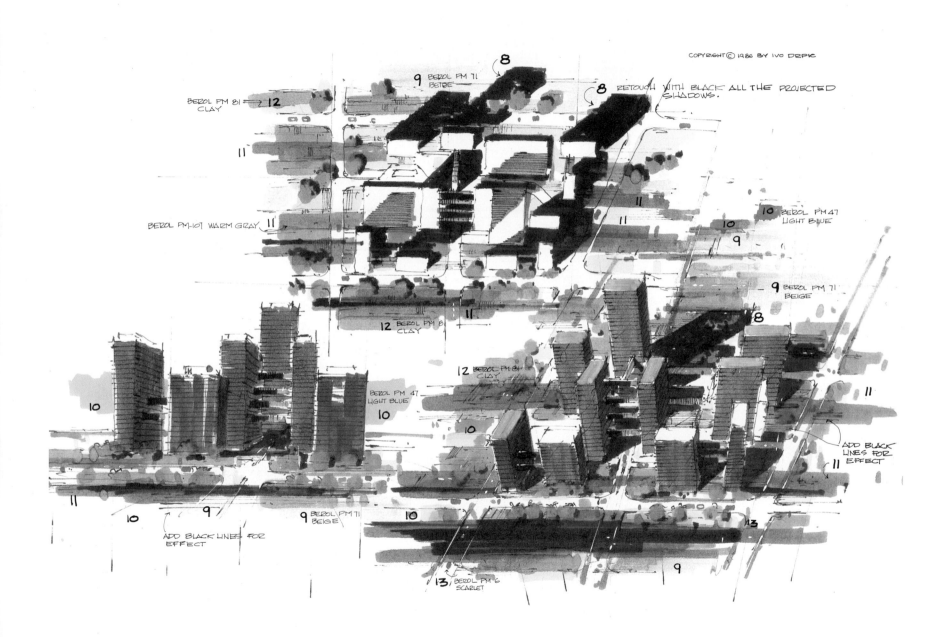

8☐ DEMONSTRATION THREE

A House Depicted from an Eye-Level View

This view is depicted as if seen from a short distance and therefore contains more details.

1. Roughly sketch the house.
2. Determine which areas are lighted and which are shaded.

3. Apply color to the roof (PM 63 Dark Brown).
4. Apply color to the shaded walls (PM 84 Bark).
5. Apply color to the glass (PM 63 Dark Brown, and PM 98 Black).
6. Apply color to the stone walls (PM 104 Warm Gray—60%, PM 100 Warm Gray—20%).
7. Color the rocks with PM 104 Warm Gray—60%, PM 100 Warm Gray—20%, and touches of black.
8. Apply vertical strokes to water (PM 47 Light Blue).
9. Apply color to the landscape (PM 36 Lime Green).
10. Mix the colors of the windows, as shown, with the thin tip of the marker (PM 63 Dark Brown).

11. Apply black (PM 98) as shadow under the roof.
12. Apply gray strokes to the rocks, using the thin tip of a Berol Prismacolor marker (PM 104 Warm Gray—60%).
13. Reinforce colors where necessary.

14. Add Olive Green (PM 34) to the landscape and apply some black touches.
15. Add vertical strokes of PM 80 Putty to the floor.
16. Mix with the thin tip of the olive colored marker, then the green, and the black.

17. Add shadows to the stone walls with PM 107 Warm Gray—90% marker.
18. Touch up the stone wall and the rocks with gray (approximately 90%).
19. Add vertical strokes of Warm Gray (PM 101) to the floor and mix with Putty (PM 80).
20. Add horizontal strokes of Warm Gray (PM 101) to the floor.

21. Add Non-Photo Blue (PM 48) to the sky.
22. Apply Warm Gray—90% (PM 107) to the shaded side of the roof.
23. Add black touches to the floor and landscape.
24. Add Non-Photo Blue (PM 48) to water to soften color.
25. Sketch trees and add color (PM 34 Olive Green) to trees, grass, and bushes.

26. Touch up entire sketch with quick strokes of a thin marker.
27. Touch up glass with terra cotta, yellow, and white markers.
28. Touch up background with yellow and terra cotta marker or pencil.
29. Apply vertical strokes with white, thin marker or tempera.
30. Add red touches sparingly.
31. Touch up with a black Sharpie marker to reinforce weak areas in the sketch.
32. Finally, add touches of Teal Blue (PM 38) to the water.

🄸 **DEMONSTRATION FOUR**

An Eye-Level View of High-Rise Buildings

This demonstration depicts high-rise buildings as seen from a short distance away. Particular attention is paid to the representation of glass for windows.

1. Work the lighted areas first. Apply Teal Blue (PM 38) to the glass of the building, leaving some blank areas as shown.
2. Apply white marker to the columns.
3. Apply Olive Green (PM 34) to landscaped areas.
4. Apply Fathom Blue (PM 41) to the sides of buildings that are in shadow.

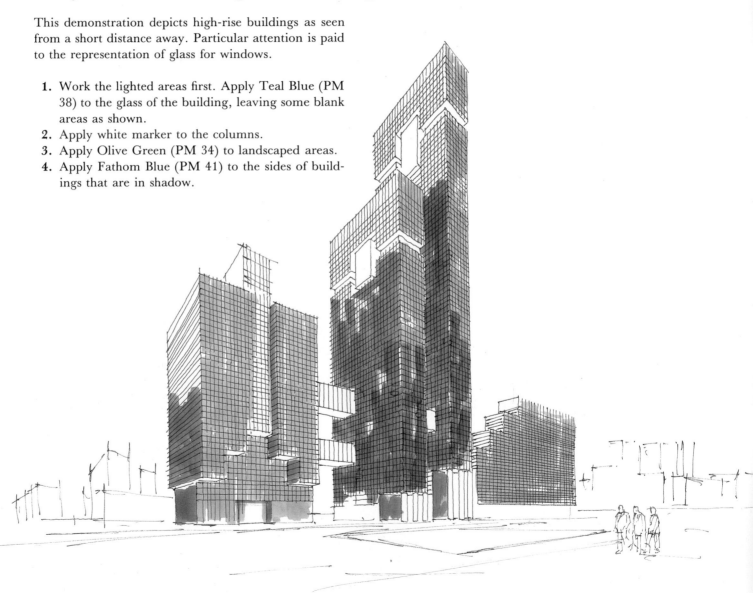

5. Make quick sketches of people in the foreground for scale.
6. Apply black to the lower part of the buildings. (Distinguish between lighted and shaded areas.)
7. With vertical strokes of Teal Blue (PM 38), mix colors in the lighted areas as shown. The same vertical strokes apply to the shaded areas. Be sure to mix the colors, but do not overwork them.
8. Apply Flagstone Red (PM 73) and Lavender (PM 59) to the water fountain.
9. Apply vertical strokes to the floor by mixing Warm Gray—50% (PM 103), Teal Blue (PM 38), and Fathom Blue (PM 41).

10. Use markers, Prismacolor pencils, or Tempera to apply touches of white, orange, yellow-red, and lilac as shown.
11. Apply final touches by adding spots of white tempera where shown.

PART IV

PORTFOLIO OF ARCHITECTURAL SKETCHES

10. HOUSING

Residence of Mr. & Mrs. Ivo D. Drpic—Bolivia. Architect:
Ivo D. Drpic. Colored markers. 24″ × 9″. 2 hours.

Sweetwater Oaks—Houston, Texas. Architect: Ivo D. Drpic
& Associates. Colored markers. 24″ × 7½″. 1¼ hours.

Sweetwater Oaks—Houston, Texas. Architect: Ivo D. Drpic
& Associates. Colored markers. 24″ × 7½″. 1¼ hours.

Sandalwood Condominiums—Houston, Texas. Architect:
Ivo D. Drpic & Associates. Colored markers. $9\frac{1}{2}'' \times 8''$.
$1\frac{1}{2}$ hours.

"The Lodge"—Walden on Lake Conroe. Architect: R & A
Architects, AIA. Colored markers. 26″ × 6½″. 2 hours.

Southpoint—Boca Raton, Florida. Architect: Ivo D. Drpic
& Associates. Colored markers on sketch paper. 18″ ×
24″. 2 hours.

Oak Grove—Houston, Texas. Architect: Ivo D. Drpic &
Associates. Colored markers. 28″ × 7½″. 2 hours.

Oak Grove—Houston, Texas. Architect: Ivo D. Drpic &
Associates. Colored markers on sketch paper. 25″ × 7½″.
2 hours.

"Las Colinas"—Bolivia. Architect: Ivo D. Drpic. Colored
markers on sketch paper. 23″ × 13″. 2 hours.

Oak Grove—Houston, Texas. Architect: Ivo D. Drpic &
Associates. Colored markers and nylon-tip pen. 26″ ×
9½″. 2 hours.

Harbor Village Condominiums—Walden on Lake Conroe.
Architect: R & A Architects, AIA. Colored markers and
nylon-tip pen. 15½″ × 6½″. 1½ hours.

Harbor Village Condominiums—Walden on Lake Conroe.
Architect: R & A Architects, AIA. Colored markers and
nylon-tip pen. 12″ × 11″. 1½ hours.

Harbor Village Condominiums—Walden on Lake Conroe.
Architect: R & A Architects, AIA. Colored markers and
nylon-tip pen. 10½″ × 8½″. 1½ hours.

Condominiums—Miami, Florida. Architect: Ivo D. Drpic &
Associates. Colored markers and nylon-tip pen. 30″ × 18″.
10 hours.

The Huntingdon—Houston, Texas. Architect: Talbott
Wilson & Associates. Colored markers and nylon-tip pen.
15½″ × 15″. 4 hours.

Condominiums—Architect: Ivo D. Drpic & Associates.
Sketch by Jeancarla Drpic. Colored markers and nylon-tip
pen. 10½″ × 8″. 2½ hours.

The Huntingdon—Houston, Texas. Architect: Talbott
Wilson & Associates. Colored markers and nylon-tip pen.
15″ × 16″. 4½ hours.

Condominiums—Maui, Hawaii. Architect: Ivo D. Drpic &
Associates. Colored markers and nylon-tip pen. 23″ ×
12½″. 5 hours.

Condominiums—Honolulu, Hawaii. Architect: Ivo D.
Drpic & Associates. Colored markers and nylon-tip pen.
15½″ × 10″. 2½ hours.

11. OFFICE BUILDINGS

Office Tower—Houston, Texas. Architect: Ivo D. Drpic &
Associates. Colored markers and nylon-tip pen. 11½″ ×
13″. 2 hours.

Office Tower—Houston, Texas. Architect: Ivo D. Drpic &
Associates. Colored markers and nylon-tip pen. 15″ × 15″.
1 hour.

Office Tower—Houston, Texas. Architect: Ivo D. Drpic &
Associates. Colored markers and nylon-tip pen. 30 minutes.

Office Tower—Houston, Texas. Architect: Ivo D. Drpic &
Associates. Colored markers and nylon-tip pen. 14½″ ×
14″. 2 hours.

Office Tower—Houston, Texas. Architect: Ivo D. Drpic & Associates. Colored markers and nylon-tip pen. 16½″ × 9½″. 1½ hours.

Office Tower—Houston, Texas. Architect: Ivo D. Drpic &
Associates. Colored markers and nylon-tip pen. 17½″ ×
18″. 1½ hours.

Office Tower—Houston, Texas. Architect: Ivo D. Drpic &
Associates. Colored markers and nylon-tip pen. 13″ ×
11½″. 30 minutes.

Office Tower—Houston, Texas. Architect: Ivo D. Drpic &
Associates. Colored markers and nylon-tip pen. 17″ ×
8½″. 20 minutes.

Office Tower—Houston, Texas. Architect: Ivo D. Drpic &
Associates. Colored markers and nylon-tip pen. 16″ × 9″.
15 minutes.

Office Tower—Cochabamba, Bolivia. Architect: Ivo D.
Drpic. Colored markers and nylon-tip pen. 12″ × 10″. 25
minutes.

J. Ray McDermott Office Complex—Houston, Texas.
Project Architects: Jack M. Reber & Ivo D. Drpic. Colored
markers and nylon-tip pen. 27″ × 7″. 2 hours.

Top: J. Ray McDermott Office Complex—Houston, Texas. Project Architects: Jack M. Reber, Ivo D. Drpic. Colored markers and nylon-tip pen. 12″ × 5″. 15 minutes.

Bottom: J. Ray McDermott Office Complex—Houston, Texas. Project Architects: Jack M. Reber, Ivo D. Drpic. Colored markers and nylon-tip pen. 11″ × 5″. 15 minutes.

Office Buildings **85**

J. Ray McDermott Office Complex—Houston, Texas.
Project Architects: Jack M. Reber, Ivo D. Drpic. Colored
markers, nylon-tip pen, and airbrush. 20 hours.

Office Complex—Houston, Texas. Architect: Ivo D. Drpic
& Associates. Colored markers and nylon-tip pen. 20″ ×
9″. 1½ hours.

Heritage Plaza—Houston, Texas. Developer: Wortham Van
Liew. Architect: M. Nasr & Partners P.C. Colored markers
and nylon-tip pen. 14″ × 16″. 8 hours.

Heritage Plaza—Houston, Texas. Developer: Wortham Van
Liew. Architect: M. Nasr & Partners, P.C. Colored
markers and nylon-tip pen. 15″ × 12″. 8 hours.

Heritage Plaza—Houston, Texas. Developer: Wortham Van
Liew. Architect: M. Nasr & Partners, P.C. Colored
markers and nylon-tip pen. 16½″ × 11″. 8½ hours.

Y.M.C.A. Project—Denver, Colorado. Developer: Nuwest,
Inc. Architect: M. Nasr & Partners, P.C. Colored markers
and nylon-tip pen. 20″ × 11½″. 4 hours.

Y.M.C.A. Project—Denver, Colorado. Developer: Nuwest,
Inc. Architect: M. Nasr & Partners, P.C. Colored markers
and nylon-tip pen. 20″ × 8½″. 50 minutes.

Mountain Tower, Nieman Co.—Glenndale, Colorado.
Architect: M. Nasr & Partners, P.C. Colored markers and
nylon-tip pen. 15″ × 12½″. 2 hours.

World Trade Center Hotel—Glendale, Colorado.
Developer: David Johnson. Architect: M. Nasr & Partners,
P.C. Colored markers and nylon-tip pen. 15″ × 11″.
2½ hours.

1220 Augusta Office Bldg. Architect: Landmark Architects, Inc. Colored markers and nylon-tip pen. 26½″ × 13″. 3 hours.

Shell Development Company

lan
Lockwood Andrews
& Newnam Inc.

Conference Facility, Shell Westhollow R & D—Houston,
Texas. Architect: Lockwood, Andrews, Newnam, Inc.
Colored markers and nylon-tip pen. 30″ × 18″. 6 hours.

IVO DRPIC
FEB. 12-86

Marathon Oil Tower—Houston, Texas. Architect: The
Office of Pierce-Goodwin-Alexander. Colored markers and
nylon-tip pen. 20″ × 15″. 4 hours.

Marathon Oil Tower—Houston, Texas. Architect: The
Office of Pierce-Goodwin-Alexander. Colored markers and
nylon-tip pen. 18″ × 13″. 4½ hours.

Fame City—Houston, Texas. Architect: The Office of
Pierce-Goodwin-Alexander. Colored markers and nylon-tip
pen. 29″ × 13″. 5 hours.

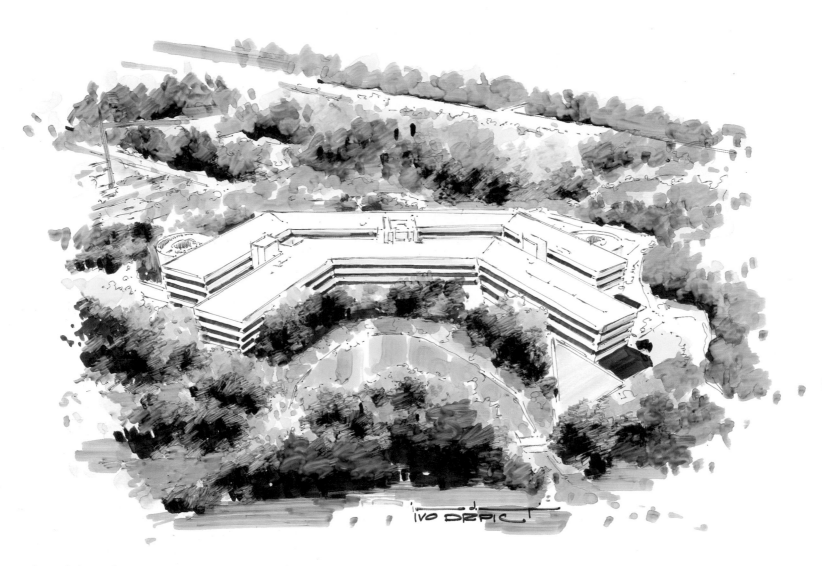

EXXON Chemical Americas—Houston, Texas. Architect:
The Office of Pierce-Goodwin-Alexander. Colored markers
and nylon-tip pen. 16″ × 10″. 1½ hours.

Brookhollow Center—San Antonio, Texas. A Development
of The Vantage Companies. Architect: Robert F.
Mitchamore. Colored markers and nylon-tip pen. 30″ ×
18″. 7 hours.

Northwest Office Park (Phase II and III)—San Antonio,
Texas. A Development of The Vantage Companies.
Architect: Robert F. Mitchamore. Colored markers and
nylon-tip pen. 30″ × 20″. 8 hours.

Office Tower—Architect: Ivo D. Drpic & Associates.
Colored markers and nylon-tip pen. 22″ × 34½″. 14
hours.

12. HOTELS, RESORTS, MARINAS

Harbor View—Walden on Lake Conroe. Developer:
Deutser & Weil. Architect: R & A Architects, AIA. Colored
markers and nylon-tip pen. 47″ × 10″. 6 hours.

Ship Store—Walden on Lake Conroe. Developer: Deutser &
Weil. Architect: R & A Architects, AIA. Colored markers
and nylon-tip pen. 13″ × 9″. 50 minutes.

The Harbors—Corpus Christi, Texas. Developer: Couch
Mortgage. Architect: Ivo D. Drpic & Associates. Colored
markers and nylon-tip pen. 29″ × 6″. 7 hours.

Hotel/Resort—South Padre Island, Texas. Architect: Ivo D.
Drpic & Associates. Colored markers and nylon-tip pen.
38″ × 12″. 2½ hours.

Condominiums—Florida. Architect: Ivo D. Drpic &
Associates. Colored markers and nylon-tip pen. 11″ × 10″.
15 minutes.

Condominiums—Florida. Architect: Ivo D. Drpic &
Associates. Colored markers and nylon-tip pen. 12″ × 12″
1½ hours.

Hotel/Resort—Chapare, Bolivia. Architect: Ivo D. Drpic.
Colored markers and nylon-tip pen. 41″ × 15″. 3½ hours.

Condominiums—San Luis Pass, Texas. Architect: Ivo D. Drpic & Associates. Colored markers and nylon-tip pen. 30″ × 15″. 2 hours.

Resort/Hotel—South Padre Island, Texas. Developer:
Cobol. Architect: Ivo D. Drpic & Associates. Colored
markers and nylon-tip pen. 29″ × 8″. 2 hours.

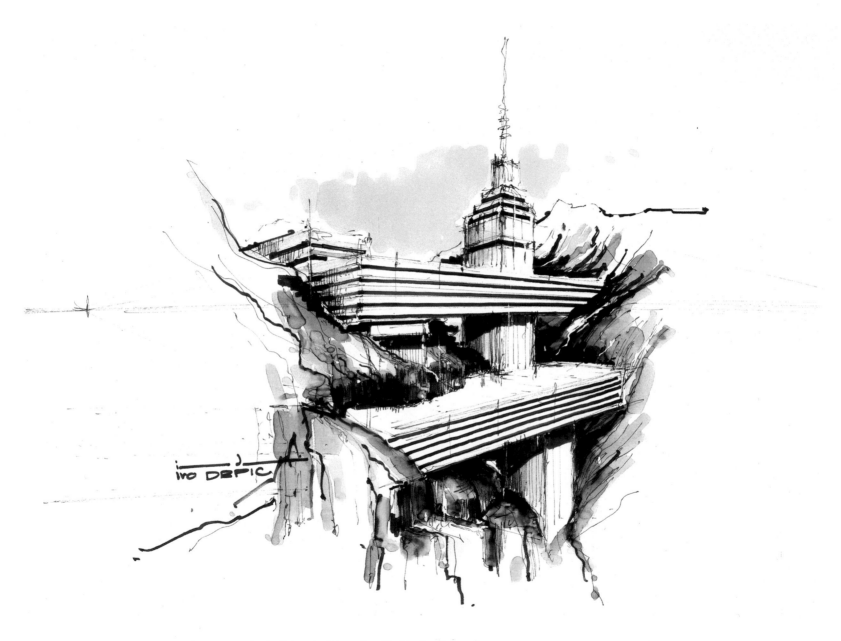

Resort Hotel—Bolivia. Architect: Ivo D. Drpic. Colored
markers and nylon-tip pen. 20″ × 13″. 15 minutes.

Resort Hotel—Bolivia. Architect: Ivo D. Drpic. Colored
markers and nylon-tip pen. 18″ × 10″. 15 minutes.

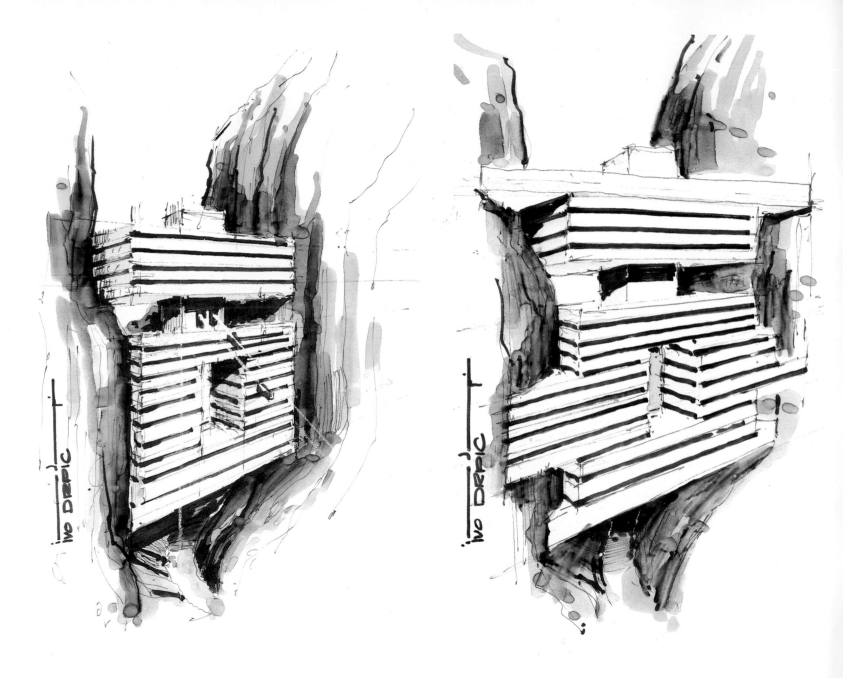

Resort Hotel— Bolivia. Architect: Ivo D. Drpic. Colored markers and nylon-tip pen. 18″ × 13″. 15 minutes.

Resort Hotel—Bolivia. Architect: Ivo D. Drpic. Colored markers and nylon-tip pen. 7″ × 11″. 15 minutes.

Condominiums—Florida. Architect: Ivo D. Drpic &
Associates. Colored markers and nylon-tip pen. 18″ × 18″.
50 minutes.

Resort Hotel—Florida. Developer: C.B.I. Architect: Ivo D.
Drpic & Associates. Colored markers and nylon-tip pen.
24″ × 9″. 1½ hours.

Resort/Hotel—Florida. Developer: C.B.I. Architect: Ivo D.
Drpic & Associates. Colored markers and nylon-tip pen.
24″ × 9″. 1 hour.

13. CHURCHES

Iglesia del Sagrado Corazon—Bolivia. Architect: Ivo D.
Drpic. Colored markers and nylon-tip pen. 15″ × 11″.
1 hour.

Iglesia de San Cirilo—Bolivia. Architect: Ivo D. Drpic.
Colored markers and nylon-tip pen. 22″ × 12″. 30
minutes.

St. Albert Catholic Church—Houston, Texas. Architect:
R & A Architects, AIA. Colored markers and nylon-tip pen.
25″ × 9½″. 2½ hours.

Iglesia de San Jose—Bolivia. Architect: Ivo D. Drpic.
Colored markers and nylon-tip pen. 10″ × 13½″. 1 hour.

Iglesia de la Santisima Cruz—Bolivia. Architect: Ivo D. Drpic. Colored markers and nylon-tip pen. 20″ × 8½″. 30 minutes.

Iglesia Catolica Los Diez Mandamientos—Bolivia.
Architect: Ivo D. Drpic. Colored markers and nylon-tip
pen. 22″ × 8½″. 50 minutes.

14. BANKS

Fondren National Bank—Houston, Texas. Architect: R & A
Architects, AIA. Colored markers and nylon-tip pen. 30″
× 18″. 2½ hours.

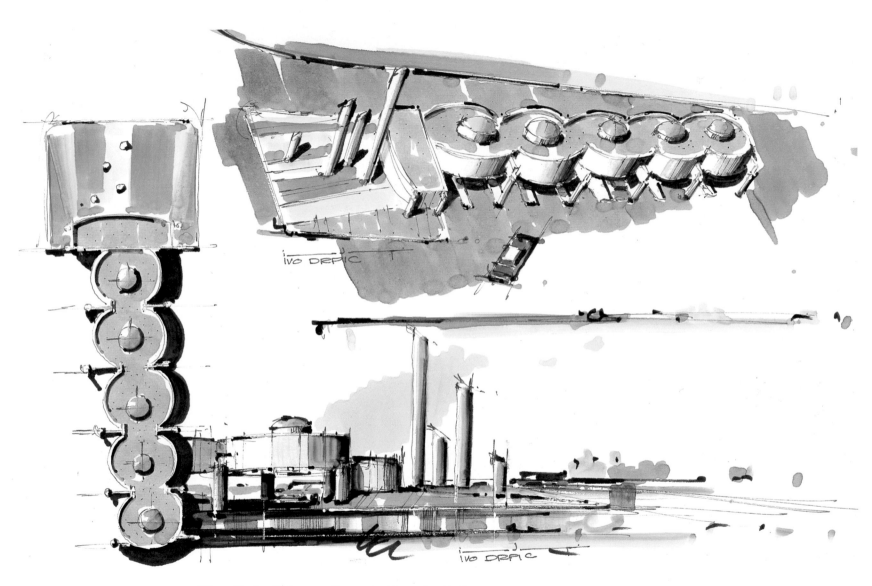

Motor Bank—Galveston, Texas. Architect: Ivo D. Drpic &
Associates. Colored markers and nylon-tip pen. 15″ × 10″.
40 minutes.

15. NURSING HOMES

The Hampton of Florida—Ft. Lauderdale, Florida.
Architect: R & A Architects, AIA. Colored markers and
nylon-tip pen. 19″ × 13″. 2 hours

Congregate Care Project—Houston, Texas. Architect:
Harold Goldstein. Colored markers and nylon-tip pen.

Morris & Frieda Wolfe Day Health Care Center—Houston,
Texas. Architect: R & A Architects, AIA. Colored markers
and nylon-tip pen. 41″ × 13″. 1½ hours.

Morris & Frieda Wolfe Day Health Care Center—Houston,
Texas. Architect: R & A Architects, AIA. Colored markers
and nylon-tip pen. 41″ × 13″. 8 hours.

16. SHOPPING CENTERS

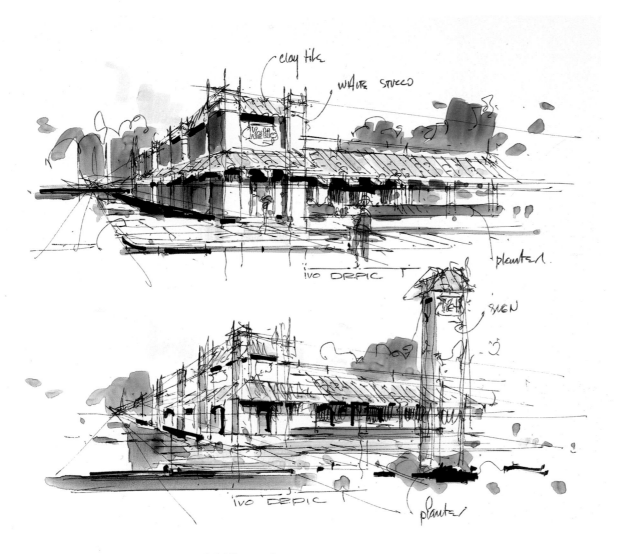

Kettle Restaurants, Inc. Architect: Paul Addington &
Associates. Colored markers and nylon-tip pen. 10″ × 14″.
10 minutes.

Kettle Restaurants, Inc. Architect: Paul Addington &
Associates. Colored markers and nylon-tip pen. 10″ × 14″.
3 hours.

Cafeteria—Houston, Texas. Architect: Ivo D. Drpic &
Associates. Colored markers and nylon-tip pen. 20″ × 7″.
1 hour.

Century Business Plaza—Houston, Texas. Architect: R & A
Architects, AIA. Colored markers and nylon-tip pen. 23″
× 5½″. 1½ hours.

Shopping Center—Houston, Texas. Architect: Ivo D. Drpic
& Associates. Colored markers and nylon-tip pen. 15″ ×
8½″. 30 minutes.

Service Center—Houston, Texas. Architect: Ivo D. Drpiċ &
Associates. Colored markers and nylon-tip pen. 17″ ×
7½″. 30 minutes.

Shopping Center—Houston, Texas. Architect: Ivo D. Drpic
& Associates. Colored markers and nylon-tip pen. 23″ ×
8″. 40 minutes.

Humble Shopping Center—Houston, Texas. Architect: Ivo
D. Drpic & Associates. Colored markers and nylon-tip pen.
14½″ × 5″. 30 minutes.

"Pueblo Viejo" Shopping Center—Houston, Texas.
Architect: Ivo D. Drpic & Associates. Colored markers and
nylon-tip pen. 14½″ × 7½″. 30 minutes.

"Pueblo Viejo" Shopping Center—Houston, Texas.
Architect: Ivo D. Drpic & Associates. Colored markers and
nylon-tip pen. 14″ × 7½″. 20 minutes.

"Los Campanarios" Shopping Center—Houston, Texas.
Architect: Ivo D. Drpic & Associates. Colored markers and
nylon-tip pen. 24″ × 12″ 4 hours.

Shopping Center. Developer: L.S.I.
Colored markers and nylon-tip pen. 30″ × 18″. 6 hours.

Shopping Center. Developer: L.S.I.
Colored markers and nylon-tip pen. 30″ × 18″. 6 hours.

Shopping Center. Developer: L.S.I.
Colored markers and nylon-tip pen. 30″ × 18″. 5 hours.

MIDTOWN CENTRE   Albany, Georgia

harold s. goldstein, architect   houston, texas

Midtown Center—Albany, Georgia. Developer: George
Reid. Architect: Harold Goldstein. Colored markers and
nylon-tip pen. 30″ × 18″. 6 hours.

Midtown Center—Albany, Georgia. Developer: George
Reid. Architect: Harold Goldstein. Colored markers and
nylon-tip pen. 20″ × 18″. 2½ hours.

Midtown Center—Albany, Georgia. Developer: George
Reid. Architect: Harold Goldstein. Colored markers and
nylon-tip pen. 20″ × 18″. 2½ hours.

MIDTOWN CENTRE   Albany, Georgia

harold s. goldstein, architect   houston, texas

Midtown Center—Albany, Georgia. Developer: George
Reid. Architect: Harold Goldstein. Colored markers and
nylon-tip pen. 30″ × 18″. 6 hours.

Three Points Common Retail Center—Austin, Texas.
Developer: Vantage Companies. Architect: Hermes, Reed,
& Hindman. Designer: Marc E. Boucher. Colored markers
and nylon-tip pen. 30″ × 18″. 7 hours.

Three Points Common Retail Center—Austin, Texas.
Developer: Vantage Companies. Architect: Hermes, Reed,
& Hindman. Designer: Marc E. Boucher. Colored markers
and nylon-tip pen. 30″ × 18″. 7 hours.

17. MULTIPURPOSE BUILDINGS

Office Building—Austin, Texas. Developer: L.S.I.
Architect: Melton-Henry. Colored markers and nylon-tip
pen. 20″ × 30″. 6 hours.

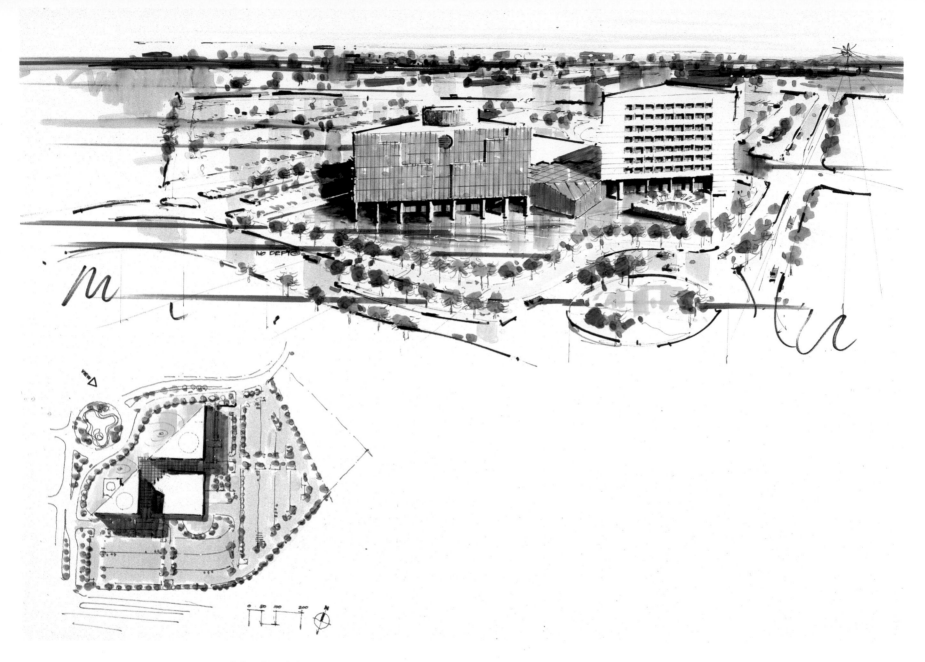

Office/Hotel/Commercial Building—Jacksonville, Florida.
Architect: Lockwood, Andrews, & Newnam, Inc. Colored
markers and nylon-tip pen. 20″ × 18″. 2 hours.

Office Building/Condominiums—Houston, Texas. Architect:
Ivo D. Drpic & Associates. Colored markers and nylon-tip
pen. 30″ × 18″. 20 hours.

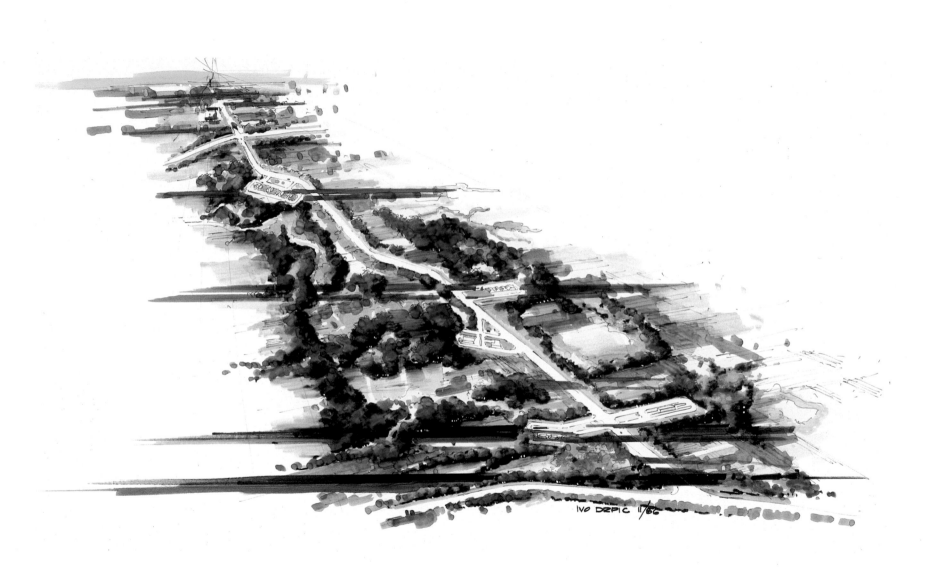

30 Acres Airfield Pavements—Gray Army Airfield, Texas.
Dietrich Engineers Incorporated. Colored markers and
nylon-tip pen. 20″ × 18″. 4 hours.

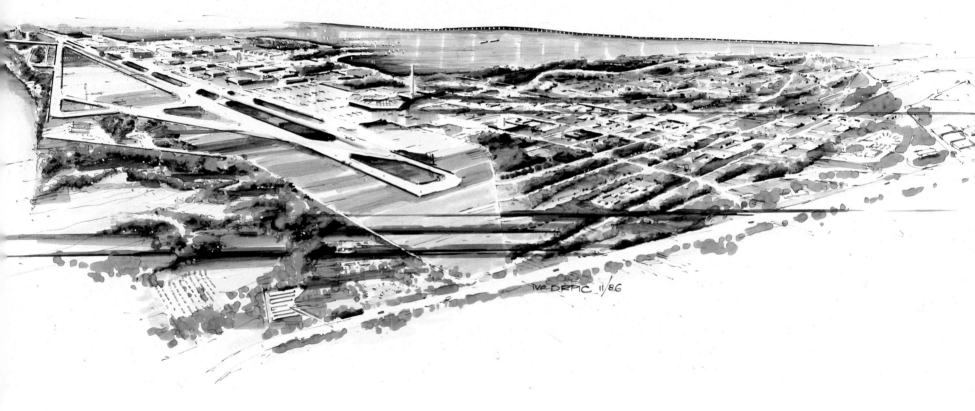

Environmental Assessment Cogeneration Plant—
Jacksonville, Florida. Dietrich Engineers Incorporated.
Colored markers and nylon-tip pen. 30″ × 18″.
6 hours.

Top: Office/Hotel/Commercial Building—Jacksonville, Florida. Architect; Lockwood, Andrews, & Newnam, Inc. Colored markers and nylon-tip pen. 20″ × 30″. 2 hours.

Bottom: Three Miles Base Roads, Five Industrial Sites, Trident Submarine Base—Kingsbay, Georgia. Dietrich Engineers Incorporated. Colored markers and nylon-tip pen. 30″ × 18″. 6½ hours.

Construction Management, Westpark Thoroughfare, Six
Lanes, Metro/City—Houston, Texas. Architect: Dietrich
Engineers Incorporated. Colored markers and nylon-tip
pen. 20″ × 18″. 4 hours.

18. CAMPUS BUILDINGS

College Expansion—Houston, Texas. Architect: Ivo D.
Drpic & Associates. Colored markers and nylon-tip pen.
31″ × 14″. 4 hours.

College Expansion—Houston, Texas. Architect: Ivo D.
Drpic & Associates. Colored markers and nylon-tip pen.
32″ × 11½″. 4½ hours.

College Expansion—Houston, Texas. Architect: Ivo D.
Drpic & Associates. Colored markers and nylon-tip pen.
25″ × 9½″. 4 hours.

University Campus Building—Houston, Texas. Architect:
Ivo D. Drpic & Associates. Colored markers and nylon-tip
pen. 13″ × 6″. 20 minutes.

University Campus Building—Houston, Texas. Architect:
Ivo D. Drpic & Associates. Colored markers and nylon-tip
pen. 13″ × 6″. 20 minutes.

University Campus Building—Houston, Texas. Architect:
Ivo D. Drpic & Associates. Colored markers and nylon-tip
pen. 12″ × 7½″. 30 minutes.

College Expansion—Houston, Texas. Architect: Ivo D.
Drpic & Associates. Colored markers and nylon-tip pen.
36″ × 13″. 2½ hours.

College Expansion—Houston, Texas. Architect: Ivo D.
Drpic & Associates. Colored markers and nylon-tip pen.
36″ × 12″. 4 hours.

College Expansion—Houston, Texas. Architect: Ivo D.
Drpic & Associates. Colored markers and nylon-tip pen.
31″ × 15″. 4 hours.

College Expansion—Houston, Texas. Architect: Ivo D.
Drpic & Associates. Colored markers and nylon-tip pen.
31½″ × 13″. 4½ hours.

College Expansion—Houston, Texas. Architect: Ivo D.
Drpic & Associates. Colored markers and nylon-tip pen.
38″ × 18″. 1½ hours.

College Expansion—Houston, Texas. Architect: Ivo D.
Drpic & Associates. Colored markers and nylon-tip pen.
36″ × 14″. 1 hour.

College Expansion—Houston, Texas. Architect: Ivo D.
Drpic & Associates. Colored markers and nylon-tip pen.
15″ × 8″. 1 hour.

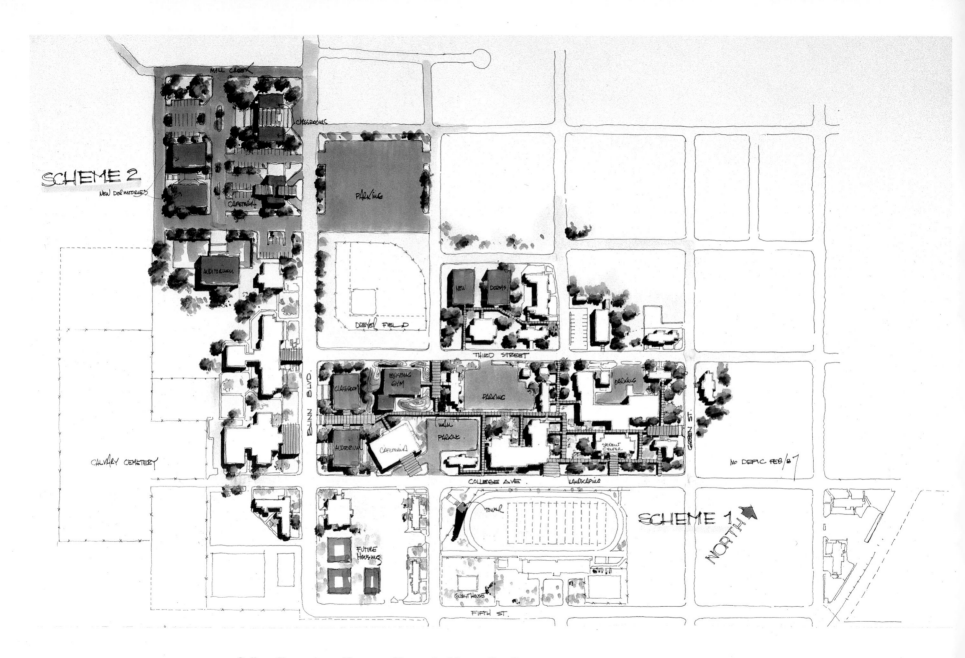

College Expansion—Houston, Texas. Architects: Ivo D.
Drpic & Associates, Jack M. Reber. Colored markers and
nylon-tip pen. 34″ × 6½″. 7 hours.

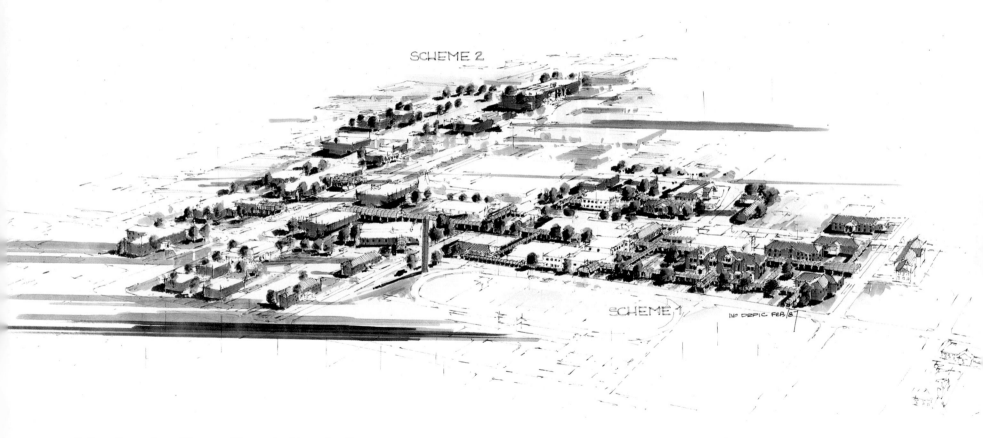

SCHEME 2

SCHEME 1

IVO DRPIC FEB/8

College Expansion—Houston, Texas. Architect: Ivo D.
Drpic & Associates. Colored markers and nylon-tip pen.
48″ × 15½″. 12 hours.

19. MEDICAL BUILDINGS

Memorial Southeast Replacement Hospital—Houston,
Texas. Architect: The Falick/Klein Partnership, Inc.
Director of Design: Barry Bruce. Colored markers and
nylon-tip pen. 17″ × 6″. 30 minutes.

Memorial Southeast Replacement Hospital—Houston,
Texas. Architect: The Falick/Klein Partnership, Inc.
Director of Design: Barry Bruce. Colored markers and
nylon-tip pen. 17″ × 6″. 1 hour.

Memorial Southeast Replacement Hospital—Houston,
Texas. Architect: The Falick/Klein Partnership, Inc.
Director of Design: Barry Bruce. Colored markers and
nylon-tip pen. 30″ × 18″. 14 hours.

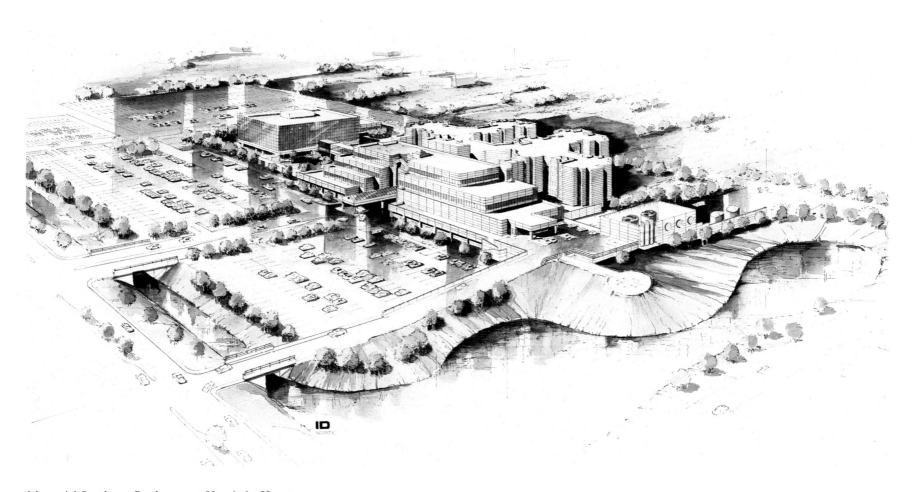

Memorial Southeast Replacement Hospital—Houston,
Texas. Architect: The Falick/Klein Partnership, Inc.
Director of Design: Barry Bruce. Colored markers and
nylon-tip pen. 30″ × 18″. 14 hours.

Memorial Southeast Replacement Hospital—Houston,
Texas. Architect: The Falick/Klein Partnership, Inc.
Director of Design: Barry Bruce. Colored markers and
nylon-tip pen. 30″ × 18″. 14 hours.

Memorial Southeast Replacement Hospital—Houston,
Texas. Architect: The Falick/Klein Partnership, Inc.
Director of Design: Barry Bruce. Colored markers and
nylon-tip pen. 20″ × 15″. 4 hours.

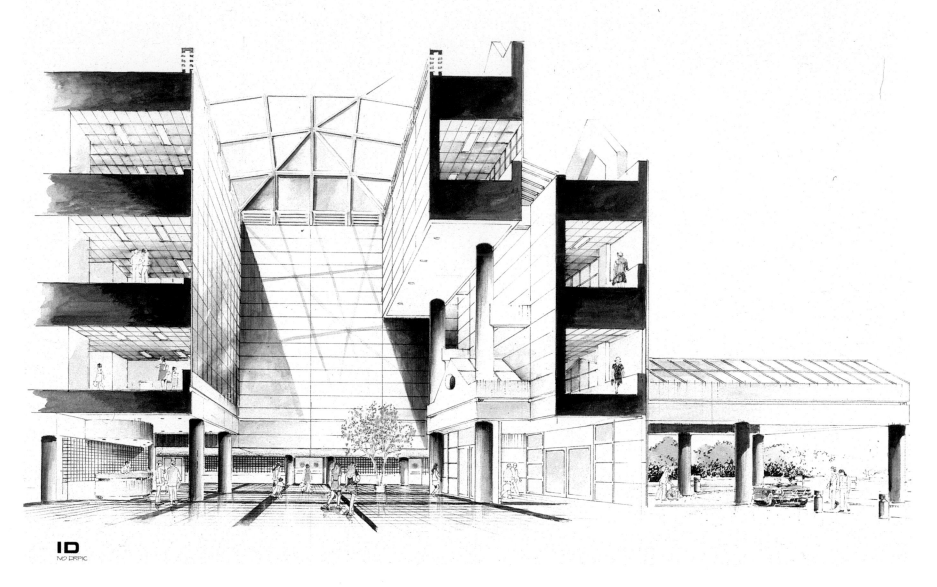

Memorial Southeast Replacement Hospital—Houston,
Texas. Architect: The Falick/Klein Partnership, Inc.
Director of Design: Barry Bruce. Colored markers and
nylon-tip pen. 17″ × 6″. 6 hours.

180 PORTFOLIO OF ARCHITECTURAL SKETCHES

Irvine Medical Center—Irvine, California. Architect: The
Falick/Klein Partnership, Inc. Director of Design: Barry
Bruce. Colored markers and nylon-tip pen. 24½″ × 7″. 6
hours.

Clinic for Upper Peninsula of Michigan. Architect: The
Falick/Klein Partnership, Inc. Director of Design: Barry
Bruce. Colored markers and nylon-tip pen. 17½″ × 6″,
18″ × 5½″, 16½″ × 4½″. 20 minutes.

Clinic for Upper Peninsula of Michigan. Architect: The
Falick/Klein Partnership, Inc. Director of Design: Barry
Bruce. Colored markers and nylon-tip pen. 17½″ × 6″,
18″ × 5½″, 16½″ × 4½″. 20 minutes.

Clinic for Upper Peninsula of Michigan. Architect: The
Falick/Klein Partnership, Inc. Director of Design: Barry
Bruce. Colored markers and nylon-tip pen. 17½″ × 6″,
18″ × 5½″, 16½″ × 4½″. 20 minutes.

Clinic for Upper Peninsula of Michigan. Architect: The
Falick/Klein Partnership, Inc. Director of Design: Barry
Bruce. Colored markers and nylon-tip pen. 16½″ × 6″. 20
minutes.

Clinic for Upper Peninsula of Michigan. Architect: The
Falick/Klein Partnership, Inc. Director of Design: Barry
Bruce. Colored markers and nylon-tip pen. 16½″ × 6″. 20
minutes.

Clinic for Upper Peninsula of Michigan. Architect: The
Falick/Klein Partnership, Inc. Director of Design: Barry
Bruce. Colored markers and nylon-tip pen. 16½″ × 6″. 20
minutes.

Shriner Hospital—Houston, Texas. Architect: Bernard
Johnson, Inc. Project Director: W. E. Ferro, AIA. Colored
markers and nylon-tip pen. 40″ × 12″. 5 hours.

Shriner Hospital—Houston, Texas. Architect: Bernard
Johnson, Inc. Project Director: W. E. Ferro, AIA. Colored
markers and nylon-tip pen. 30″ × 18″. 2 hours.

Shriner Hospital—Houston, Texas. Architect: Bernard
Johnson, Inc. Project Director: W. E. Ferro, AIA. Colored
markers and nylon-tip pen. 30″ × 18″. 2 hours.

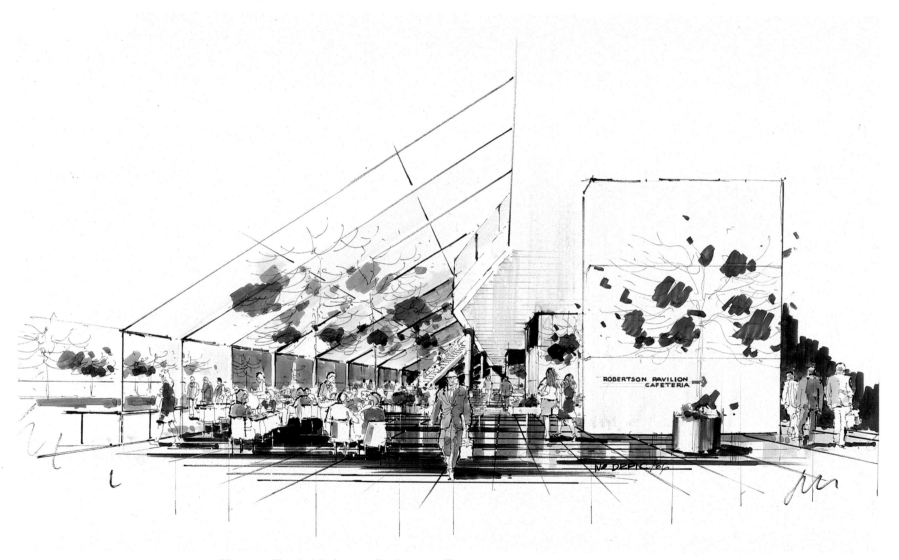

Hermann Hospital Robertson Replacement Tower—
Houston, Texas. Architect: Bernard Johnson, Inc. Project
Director: W. E. Ferro, AIA. Colored markers and nylon-tip
pen. 20″ × 18″. 2 hours.

Magnetic Resonance Imaging Facility—Marquette,
Michigan. Architect: The Falick/Klein Partnership, Inc.
Director of Design: Barry Bruce. Colored markers, nylon-
tip pen, and airbrush. 30″ × 18″. 8 hours.

Beauregard Hospital—DeRidder, Louisiana. Architect: The
Falick/Klein Partnership, Inc. Director of Design: Barry
Bruce. Colored markers, nylon-tip pen, and airbrush. 30″
× 18″. 12 hours.

Memorial Northwest Replacement Hospital—Houston, Texas. Architect: The Falick/Klein Partnership, Inc. Director of Design: Barry Bruce. Colored markers and nylon-tip pen. 20″ × 18″. 30 minutes.

Memorial Northwest Replacement Hospital—Houston,
Texas. Architect: The Falick/Klein Partnership, Inc.
Director of Design: Barry Bruce. Colored markers and
nylon-tip pen. 20″ × 18″. 30 minutes.

Memorial Northwest Replacement Hospital—Houston,
Texas. Architect: The Falick/Klein Partnership, Inc.
Director of Design: Barry Bruce. Colored markers and
nylon-tip pen. 20″ × 18″. 30 minutes.

Memorial Northwest Replacement Hospital—Houston,
Texas. Architect: The Falick/Klein Partnership, Inc.
Director of Design: Barry Bruce. Colored markers and
nylon-tip pen. 20″ × 18″. 30 minutes.

Memorial Northwest Replacement Hospital—Houston,
Texas. Architect: The Falick/Klein Partnership, Inc.
Director of Design: Barry Bruce. Colored markers and
nylon-tip pen. 20″ × 18″. 30 minutes.

Memorial Northwest Replacement Hospital—Houston,
Texas. Architect: The Falick/Klein Partnership, Inc.
Director of Design: Barry Bruce. Colored markers and
nylon-tip pen. 20″ × 18″. 30 minutes.